FIRST PUBLISHED FEBRUARY 2024

Cover art based on a painting by the author (acrylic on canvas)

Distributed by Amazon

ISBN 978-0-9812280-7-5

IS IT DARK IN THERE?

Steve Lewis

IS IT DARK IN THERE?

ANSWERS FOR CAVE DIVERS
BUT MOSTLY FOR THE CURIOUS

Dedication

Ms. Siggy, for being my rock when others turned out to be sandcastles against an incoming tide. And, by the way, that keychain that you gave me a while back, doesn't count; I love you more.

Finally, thanks for the cats, the puppy, and so much more...

Table of Contents

Acknowledgements

Certainly, thanks to everyone within earshot who has ever been curious about caves and cave diving. Especially my late father and my uncle Dave. Both of whom were filled with an infectious and childlike curiosity, always and until the very end. They never stopped asking questions. I can only hope that whatever section of paradise the two of them occupy right now, there is access to excellent coverage of Formula 1 car racing, stacks of history books, a large pile of Hovis and beef-dripping sandwiches, and endless crates of brown ale.

Getting this book to press was rudely interrupted by a diagnosis of cancer: mine. Since this isn't a biography, that in itself is of little interest except it introduced me to some remarkable people. And this seems a good time to thank them publicly.

So, thanks to Dr. Grace Ma, a gifted surgeon, and a cheeky behind the scenes administrative string-puller. She, against the odds, took me apart, threw out the wonky bit, and reassembled the leftovers close enough to brand-new not to matter. The scars are impressive. But so too is that with covid rampant, and some follow-up elective work needed, under her direction, the queue for that procedure suddenly got shortened from several months to a few days.

Also, thank you to her colleague, Dr. Sathish Gopalakrishnan (the blood test dude) my equally inspired haematologist/oncologist. Those two orchestrated the moves of an impressive team of medical folks who saved my bacon and smiled cheerily while doing so.

Sathish also suggested I read *Shantaram*, which took my mind off the horrid taste in my mouth caused by the nasty but necessary drugs he pumped into me. Thank you, and you were correct, it was worth it, and I enjoyed the book. Good luck wading through this one.

Many people were hands-on help getting this book together. Tonya Lee Castle was coffee maker, and proofer. As a newish diver – the non-cave diving kind – Tonya also helped to sense-check the text making sure I'd managed to explain most of the complex bits for a 'lay audience'.

My Limey/Australian buddy, David Strike, an author of note, and ex Fleet Street daily worker himself, was kind enough to write the foreword.

Richie Kohler, that wreck-diving guy and TV host, got hold of an advanced copy and liked it enough to put a back page blurb together for me.

Thanks to the folks at Surveydown.com for the use of a section of their excellent map of Sistema Exploradora on page 50.

There are, of course, so many more to thank. Questioners as a collective, for example.

Richard Dunbar, who you'll meet in Question One, mentioned the role of gossip in the evolution of society. He also proposed that our brains are built in such a way that we can only maintain "a stable relationship", with a maximum of around 150 people. Any greater number and identities, faces, interpersonal relationships within the group blur, fade and melt into a form on benign anonymity.

In his book, *Sapiens, A brief history of humankind,* Yuval Noah Harari uses a similar number when writing about the optimal size for a community. Accordingly, he writes that when a tribe grows beyond that 150-unit boundary, its group dynamic changes and true friendships erode. (Facebook as evidence.)

I didn't count all the people who made this book happen before writing this note, but it was many more than the 150 limit. Accordingly, I have lost track of them. Their questions about what I do to keep sane in an insane world triggered the original idea for this book.

Therefore, my hope is that this book does a better job expressing my thanks at arm's length than I could ever do face-to-face. If you are one of those wonderful people, as delightful as it would be to list you all here, I've lost track of who you all were. Apologies, but thank you all nevertheless.

Preface.

"The purpose of writing is to inflate weak ideas, obscure poor reasoning, and inhibit clarity..."
Calvin and Hobbes: Bill Watterson.

This book is intended for three types of reader: cave divers old and new; divers who may never enter a cave 'because that stuff is not for me'; but primarily for the curious who wonder what the hell drives someone to take up a pastime so bizarre and mysterious.

The questions and answers inside here aren't herded into appropriate spaces and consecutive chapters, like sheep into pens struggling and kicking. Questions and answers are not nearly as cute or woolly or as badly-behaved as sheep. And I left it up to them to line up as they pleased. What this means is the reader isn't expected to start at the beginning and finish at the end. What's inside these covers is not driven by a sequential narrative. Each question and its answer is a standalone essay. There is no storyline to follow.

However, probably good to know that the questions themselves cover general topics, which people who have nothing to do with cave diving, technical diving, or diving at all tend to ask... what's a cave, are they all the same, why on earth would you go in there, is it dangerous, and so on?

Some questions – more robust and curlier... like Lincoln Sheep... big and substantial – cover actual cave-diving protocols. My guess is these will interest divers: cave and otherwise. So, if you ever wondered how to factor a stage bottle into your gas calculations or why a crescent wrench (adjustable spanner) and a cable-tie can be essential 1200 metres back in a cave; or you're not a diver at all but you'd like to know what all that nonsense means. And finally, there are questions that fall into the completely random category. Like sheep running around without fences.

Catch 'em if you can.

Steve Lewis (AKA Doppler)

Tulum, Mexico| Rosseau, Milton, and Sudbury, Ontario |
October 2022 - January 2024.

Foreword

By David Strike

Reviewing a book is made so much easier when the reviewer has, at the very least, a smidgeon of insider knowledge regarding the topic. Regrettably, pride often stands in the way when it comes to confessing one's ignorance. Which is why, in the interests of full disclosure, I have to admit that I am not, nor had I ever been, a cave diver, nor had I ever even considered cave diving as a 'must-do' activity, when, as an unashamed admirer of Steve Lewis's previous works, I was invited to preview his latest book, 'Is It Dark In There?' – a book on cave diving.

Fortunately - as I later discovered in reading the book - I'm apparently not alone in my ignorance. And while I'll happily listen to edge-of-the-seat tales of cave diving exploration told by friends and colleagues who get their rocks off (cave pun intended) by wriggling their bodies through small, dark, water-filled holes in the ground merely to discover where – if anywhere – they lead, I've never been inspired to give it a try. And that's despite having a shelf full of 'HOW TO' books on cave diving.

And therein lies the difference that sets, 'Is It Dark In There?' apart from other books of the genre: it's one that's written as much for people like me, as it is for the would-be and the already committed cave diver. And it does so, not by a sequential series of chapters focused on, 'HOW TO CAVE DIVE' (although it does delve into established protocols) but by posing - and then providing answers to – questions that range from the seemingly simple to the more complex. Including an analysis of that greatest question of all, 'WHY?'

Those answers, to even the simplest question, often follow tangential pathways leading to delightfully surprising outcomes.

A long-time technical diving instructor and active cave diver with decades of enviable experience, who, in his own words, "... has been lucky enough to enjoy messing around underwater in places as different and interesting as caves in Brazil, shipwrecks in North America's Great Lakes, and with icebergs in Canada's province of Newfoundland", Steve Lewis is, in every sense of the word, a 'Renaissance Man'; one who carries the reader through philosophical concepts while introducing them to some of literature and history's greatest figures, people whose collective wisdom has a direct bearing on the original question.

As, Steve Lewis writes, in the early pages of the book, "Questions fire the imagination; they add definition to our dreams and fan the flames of our creativity." That may be so. But it's the answers that add colour and meaning, that stimulate the desire for further knowledge and understanding, and that frequently give rise to further questions. And this is where, 'Is It Dark In There?' excels.

Rather than trivialising any of the questions posed; or, minimising the risks and dangers inherent in cave diving by avoiding the 'death' word, each receives a comprehensive and beautifully crafted answer. And in much the same way that the books opening pages describes the jungle landscape of Mexico's Yucatan Peninsula as being 'stubby', while, just a metre or so beneath the surface, lie the rivers, streams and lakes of, "the most extensive network of caves in the Americas", 'Is It Dark In There?' is filled with an unexpected treasury of knowledge and information as an answer to every question.

When asked to describe the cenotes and what they lead to, Steve Lewis wrote, "I mentioned long soda straws hanging like stone icicles, multicoloured flowstones smooth and viscous, calcite walls the colour of royal icing, and of course the forests of stalactites and stalagmites thick and organic ... it is here in the dark, a darkness that's deeper than existence itself, that one sees things very clearly. You simply have to be willing to open your mind and look, and by doing so, we will find ALL the answers to every question ever asked about the strange pastime of cave diving."

In short, 'Is It Dark In There?', has all of the hallmarks of a classic of its type, a book that begs to be read and enjoyed, time and time again. And having challenged all of my previous perceptions and misconceptions about cave diving ... and cave divers, my biggest regret is that I never had the opportunity to read and learn from it when I was setting out in diving.

Prologue

"Indistinct and inaccurate images are all that's left to us when the wild recollection of past exploits charges through the spiderweb of memory pulling it to pieces, and in the process, the warming recollections that were caught in its sticky traces are pulled away from the connective threads of consequent recall to be isolated and obscured by grey hair, and the attraction of past participles to stand alone and forlorn. And that's the sad reality of outliving one's family and too many friends. But enough of the poetry, what I mean to say is the older I get, the better I was..."

- W. Rhys Morgan.

Please be patient during your walk from the baggage carousel and customs desks to the waiting limousine. At one time, Cancun Airport was easier to navigate than now. But times have changed.

The gauntlet of hawkers selling timeshare condos, cheap taxi rides to "the best hotels" and Playa Del Carmen, are dealing and wheeling. The unconvincing wide boys fibbing to you that your pre-arranged ride has phoned in sick and cancelled, well, they are lined up three deep now, ready and waiting. Uniformed and more professionally insistent than ever, the car rental agents flogging "amazing deals," and smartly suited in-bound operators are touting seats on tourist buses to Xel-Ha, lifts to the Hard Rock Café, guided tours of Chichén Itzá, and Cenote dive packages; everyone is here.

To a person, they are annoying but slick. As competitive as Wall Street stock traders and as bent out of shape running after the tourist dollar. Don't blame them, blame the tourists dressed like surfer dudes who've had a little too much free booze on the flight in from the bleak Midwest; but beware, nevertheless. Just walk on; our driver is waiting because he did not call in sick. No, he is holding an iPad tablet with your name displayed on its screen. He has cold bottled water, chilled Corona, lemon-scented face wipes, and an air-conditioned ride waiting just the other side of the car park.

What brings us to Mexico, isn't the sun, the sand, or the tequila, not this time; it's the caves. But not here in Cancun. To arrive in that nexus, we must travel south on Highway 307, towards Belize. South through the Karst landscape of Quintana Roo. Flat and squat countryside, wild and tangled. A friend asked me once if I knew why the jungle here on Mexico's Yucatan was so "stubby." I have no idea. Perhaps though it's related to the soil. Thin, meagre, and sitting on top of a huge limestone slab that's as porous as sponge toffee. I don't know why the trees are so short, but in this whole area there is nothing approaching the security of solid ground. So, it seems logical the trees know better than to reach too far up to the sky for fear of falling over.

They know that underfoot, no matter where you go, a few metres down at most, is water, but not the type held magically in suspension and somehow locked away in the soil like a dark secret. That is the water table in other parts of the world, but not here. No, this is water undisguised. It is rivers, streams, and lakes all under the surface all in the forever-dark, and a function of a strange and fortunate chemistry.

This is cave country and just below us are a thousand portals to Xibalba, the Mayan underworld "a place of fright." But no fright for us. For us, Xibalba is a network of water filled caves calling out to be explored: a species of friends mistaken for Mayan myths.

Nothing at all supernatural, just the most extensive network of caves in the Americas. More extensive than those in Kentucky, more inviting than those in Florida's Gulf coast between the panhandle and Fort Myers.

The cave network here stretches to all horizons and beyond. East to the Gulf of Mexico but not stopping there. North to the scar of the Chicxulub crater, the extinction capital of the world all those millions of years ago. West until the next state, and south beyond the border with Belize, the English Latin America. And it's to explore those caves that we are here.

Our destination is Tulum. It is an odd town, an old fishing village that's morphed and evolved into a not-quite-regular vacation town, its personality split somehow between the Mayans, Meztecs, Mexicans, and more than ever, people from away; all of them walking its streets, and each with their own reasons for being there. This town, Tulum, will be our second home during our exploration; our base camp.

Tulum is a fishing village in transition. When I first visited, a marriage, a head of grey hair, and a career ago, it was only partway to being changed beyond recognition by visitors. It's closer now. There is a sort of guilt attached to triggering that change because we are visitors too. But we kid ourselves that we are different to the resort-dwelling tourists locked in their expensive Disneyworld compounds a few kilometers away. They don't venture out much, and seldom as far south as Tulum. Perhaps they make it to the old Mayan ruins on the northern outskirts, but not into town itself.

No, here are a different order of holidaymakers: the normal ones. Many of them Mexican, because this their Miami Beach, their Cote d'Azur, their Amalfi Coast.

Many of the others come for a couple of weeks to get away from the cold at home. They practice their Spanish, take selfies in the ice-cream parlours, eat at the cheap taco stands, pay too much for their cups of cortado, but head home happy and sun kissed.

Then there are the 'trustafarians.' The rich trust-fund kids and their buddies with beaded dreadlocks, women in cotton kaftans, men with wispy beards, hanging out on the beach road in the yoga studios, new-age cafes, and coffee shops. They stay for as long as it takes to open their chakras – sometimes longer – and depart with memories.

There are the backpackers. The western European and American kids here on the cheap to smoke dope, party on the beach, get laid, and watch to sun come up over the ocean. They stay until the new semester starts, and then head home again.

Then come the hardcore oddballs. The 'permanent aliens'. The expats. Every nationality under the sun but bonded by what's beneath their feet; the network of caves running like a sort of Marvel Comics underwater maze. These folks drive Toyota pickups filled with dive gear, they speak Spanish with unexpected accents, and they stay here to dive, to explore, to discover, and to take care of their customers.

Their customers: the final group. That's the group we belong to. This is our tribe. We are among the group who travel here specifically to visit the caves to swim in them and to marvel at what they have to show us. But there is a price.

We'll talk about that price later but be aware that it's one of those fluid costs that is completely based on attitude and our values.

Years ago, in another limo, once the driver learned I was here to dive the cenotes and the endless kilometers of caves they lead to, explained that the caves are special to his people: the Maya. He described the cenotes and caves as magical and told me to be wary of Hun-Came one of many gods waiting to in the dark to hand death to the unprepared. Unfortunately, I know of this creature. But we will talk about that later too.

When he asked me to describe the cenotes and what they lead to. I mentioned long soda straws hanging like stone icicles, multicoloured flowstones smooth and viscous, calcite walls the colour of royal icing, and of course the forests of stalactites and stalagmites thick and organic and like the Santa's Christmas grotto in some half-remembered Peckham toyshop when I was a boy. All these the result of thousands of years of rain falling on the jungle above and weaving through porous rock to satisfy gravity's pull.

I am not sure he understood me, but regardless, it is here in the dark, a darkness that's deeper than existence itself, that one sees things about the complexity of this planet, and oneself, very clearly. You simply have to be willing to open your mind and look, and by doing so, we will find ALL the answers to every question ever asked about the strange pastime of cave diving.

Question One

QUESTIONS: DOESN'T IT ALL START RIGHT THERE?

"They say there are no stupid questions. That's obviously wrong; I think my question about hard and soft things [asked to his mother when he was a youngster], for example, is pretty stupid. But it turns out that trying to thoroughly answer a stupid question can take you to some pretty interesting places."

- Randall Munroe, What If? Serious Scientific Answers to Absurd Hypothetical Questions.

Robin Dunbar argues that gossip helped early humans navigate the transition from small nomadic bands of hunter-gatherers to forming larger, cohesive groups living in permanent settlements. His contention is the intrigue of who was doing what to whom did not coincide with - but was the driving force behind - the switch from chasing bison and woolly mammoths, with flint-tipped spears, to settling into life as farmers tending crops, herding domesticated livestock, building a civilization, mowing the lawn, and wasting time by playing golf.

What Professor Dunbar is telling us is that the ability to speak and communicate complex ideas was key for frail humans to hunt big game effectively, and to survive. However, it's our hard-wired tendency to gossip that led directly to the growth of a civilization based on towns, city-states, and beyond.

Dunbar, a professor of evolutionary psychology, writes that without gossip, those early agricultural societies would have had difficulty evolving into anything more complex than a collection of tiny hamlets. In effect, without the influence of a bunch of gossips, I'd be holding a hand-knapped chunk of chert or obsidian instead of sitting at the keyboard of an Apple laptop computer.

True enough, perhaps, and foolish of me to pick a fight with an Oxford Don, but there's something else that drives us as a species and that sets Homo Sapiens apart: questions. Anyone who's spent an hour or two traveling with a three-year-old in the back seat of a car could have told him this. He should have asked!

And so, if gossip is a key ingredient to modern society's structure and growth, as Professor Dunbar states, it is questions that have added the sparkle and insight and helped to push human ingenuity. If gossip helped grow another branch on the human family tree, questions added the lights, decorations, and put the tinsel-covered star on top.

Casual conversations, complaining about the rain and late frost that took out the tomato plants, small talk about workmates who steal other people's food from the community fridge, chatting about things that are not going to change the world – all terms for gossip – frequently start with somebody asking questions.

That little kid in the back of the car driving her parents crazy is just following her nature. Human nature... questions are a sort of growth hormone for the mind, and when shared deliver a sense of belonging. Only autistic savants don't ask questions: although perhaps they do too, but we don't listen.

The best podcasts, old fashioned detective thrillers, Netflix specials, enduring poetry, the best fiction, and science are all built on a foundation of neatly arranged questions.

Questions fire the imagination; they add definition to our dreams and fan the flames of our creativity.

It turns out that cats are not the only ones who suffer from curiosity. (Although theirs can usually be satisfied by knocking whatever catches their eye off the kitchen counter and watching it drop to the floor. Evidenced by the noise coming from my kitchen now as I write this.) Thankfully, human inquisitiveness is not as easily satisfied.

Voltaire said that one should judge a man by his questions rather than his answers. So, it seems fine to tell you that questions, and what generates them, is what this book is about. Not the generic: Why is the sky blue; Why do all the houses on that street look the same; Are we there yet; Are we alone in the universe; Why do people live in Basingstoke? None of that. This collection relate in one way or the other to the specific, sublime, esoteric, mysterious, and some say, most dangerous pastime, cave diving.

As a kid, I got thoroughly muddy by crawling around in the caves of England's Mendip Hills, and any other hole in the ground big enough to wriggle into. Caves were damp, they smelled off, had very strange critters in them. Most of all, caves had me totally fascinated. I loved them. I felt at home sitting in them breathing in the age-old dreams and kept promises they held within their rock walls. And always puzzled by the occasional fossil stuck there like those awful plaster flying ducks that Aunt Doll had in her hallway in Morden.

Later, I discovered that swimming into water-filled caves wearing a drysuit and SCUBA gear or a rebreather was a whole lot easier and quieter and less muddy, and safer (more about that later). So, I started to do it instead... and I am still at it.

Because of all that, I learned whenever you do anything labelled odd or different, people ask questions. Sometimes, those questions are rhetorical because a handful of people have already made up their mind that you're batshit crazy, a buccaneer and adrenalin junkie. Any explanation or attempt to provide a reasonable answer falls on closed minds since their assessment is a freakishly wrong oversimplification.

So, in part, this is a detailed response. What follows is a personal justification to point out to those people that they are wrong.

But I know none of them is listening. Anyway, this is for you.

If you have ever wondered what makes someone travel halfway across town or around the world to crawl or swim into a hole in wet rock, this book may be of interest.

Moreover, if you are someone who travels across town or halfway around the world to disappear into a hole in a wet rock, buy several copies of this book and give them to friends and family. It may help to answer their questions and save you the trouble!

If you are an academic working on a PhD or doing post-doc work in evolutionary psychology or some other investigation into the vagaries of human nature, please add this book to your reference library.

And finally, if you're at all interested in this beautiful planet and the many secrets it still holds deep inside its corpus, and you're wondering how to spend a bunch of disposable income, or you're wondering what to do when you grow up (or instead of growing up), this book will answer questions you probably did not know you had.

Enjoy. Dive safe. Dive often. Just do it and have fun.

Question Two

"IS IT DARK IN THERE?"

- The first question from a surprising number of folks who ask about cave diving... including my uncle, Dave Maslin.

Terri Orbuch, is billed as <The Love Doctor.> She's a therapist, a relationship expert, and the author of a bunch of books pointing out what questions best elevate a conversation from small talk to "comfortable real talk." These questions, she explains, are designed to open the door to another person's "inner world."

Ever the skeptic and about as far from a relationship expert as you're likely to meet, nevertheless, I believe Dr. Orbuch is onto something. The idea that people ask questions to connect with us and our inner world is flattering. Being asked about that one thing we do to keep us sane, the crazy pastime that adds balance to our life, triggers the sharing gene in most of us. And like any enthusiast who is crazy for their favourite and unusual pastime – from breeding racing pigeons, to building popsicle-stick dioramas of Renaissance Florence, or in the case in hand, strapping on sixty kilos of dive gear and swimming into a hole in the ground – when someone asks us "Why on earth would you do that?", it gives us an opportunity to share the passion; to pull them into our inner world; to engage them in comfortable real talk. It turns out we all have something of the preacher, the proselytizer, in our make-up. And of course, we all want to justify ourselves, to let people know that we are not as reckless as we seem. Maybe.

Questions about cave diving fall into a handful of well-defined categories. The most common is the list titled, "Funny that you should ask that." These include the ubiquitous and bizarre: Is it dark in there? Do they string lights up in the cave so that people can see? How far into the cave can you go before you have to turn back because it's dark?

When a cave diver talks about a cave, what they imagine and try to describe to anyone who'll listen, is quite different to what someone asking questions from this list imagines a cave to be. And, when one answers what seem to be the silliest questions, it pays to be gracious and tactful with this in mind.

Caves are holes in solid rock. That's a good starting point. That rock is mostly limestone, which is porous, easily dissolved by slightly acidic rain, and given several thousand years and plenty of rainfall, forms the complex voids we call caves. However, since caves are essentially just holes in rock, light has a difficult time traveling through it. Mexico, the UK, the Caribbean, the US, Europe, Asia, and Australia all have caves that attract divers. And while all caves are different, and each with its own character and beauty, they share a community of similarity.

The most conspicuous is darkness.

The inside of a cave has never witnessed daylight, never seen the glow of a full moon or the eerie kiss of starlight from the Milky Way. Beyond its cavern zone – defined as the spot where the faint influence of daylight fades to black – the cave is darker than a dungeon, blacker than the river Styx, and full of a gloom deeper than the bone-carver's lair. Venturing past its cavern, a cave becomes a black hole, and at that transition from cavern to cave, one leaves a world ruled by sunlight and enters into a place where shadows and reflection are fantasies. This boundary is an event horizon, and that is exactly the spot where the fun begins. This is where the dualism of yin and yang and Carl Jung's concept of the shadow-self steps out of the darkness to greet us.

So, yes, it's dark in there. Dylan Thomas, the Welsh poet wrote about a starless, bible-black, sloeblack, slow black night. Well, caves are blacker than that.

It's said, darkness is what turned our ancestors from predator to prey. Our fear of total darkness, such a common phobia, springs from this perhaps; a primitive and archaic anxiety deeply rooted in the brain's architecture, many layers deep, and difficult to shake. When my daughter was five or six, she would get up in the middle of the night to pee in the quiet dark of the house, sure that once the bathroom light was switched off again, if she did not make it back under the sheets before the toilet finished flushing, some creature was ready to spring from the blackness to grab her.

Was hers an irrational, unfounded fear, or a hard-wired safeguard older than our species, and evolved to foil sabre-toothed cats, cave bears, and hyenas? One or the other, it doesn't matter, because in the end, the behaviour is the same. Darkness creates uncertainty.

Of course, prehistoric tigers and wild dogs don't roam suburban Unionville. Back then, the real issue was convincing her to stay in the bathroom long enough to wash her hands properly.

In any case, caves are immensely dark, and in that darkness, the vagaries of human history, the passage of time, and any hope of change is introduced only by the various high-tech underwater flashlights divers carry with them. Nothing else.

LIGHTS

By the way, there are no hanging lights installed in caves to guide divers on their adventures, and interrupt millennia of dark. There are plenty of reasons why this is an impractical, environmentally damaging, and ludicrously expensive proposition. The strings of lights would need to be kilometers long, to begin with. More importantly, this would irrevocably damage the cave, plus it would also take away one of the pleasures of cave diving: to hang motionless and suspended in the water around midway through the dive, far back and away from the world, and then to turn off one's lights, and experience blackness like no other.

One sits in the dark for a few minutes enjoying the non-scenery. Certainly not long enough to actually trigger the hallucinations that come with true sensory deprivation, but strangely invigorating, nevertheless. And actually, a minute or two into the experience, the part of one's awareness that has been bombarded with light and images since before birth, starts to react in the strangest ways. Not the intense mind-altering visions participants in Etienne Koechlin's 40 days of darkness experiments experienced but the beginnings of an odd dance of imaginary luminescence that can become addictive. Addictive enough to become a reason to cave dive. There's an odd confession.

I wonder if Palaeolithic cave painters with stories of the hunt in mind, ever covered the dim light from their tallow lamps to gather inspiration.

No matter.

There are dry caves that attract tourists, and these do have strings of permanent lights. But cave divers do their thing underwater and carry specially designed flashlights with them.

The common practice is to carry a powerful primary light and at least two or three smaller backups. So, in a team of three divers – the preferred team size according to the textbooks, if one believes what they tell us and follows their advice – the team will have at least nine lights and possibly several more, between them.

Why so careful? Well, a long swim in utter darkness, perhaps with only the faint promise of an illuminated instrument face on one's wrist to guide one's way home, is not fun, and far from the thrill of turning a light off for a few minutes to wallow in the dark knowing things can be reversed with the flick of a switch.

As a mental test and as an introduction to one's Shadow Self, there are special skills that a diver learns to become a cave diver including "lights out drills." These teach what exiting in complete darkness is like, as unlikely as that would be. Possibly, these are a legacy from when the lights we carried into caves were far less reliable, and the power supply driving them was less dependable than it is today. Back when one expected to have a minimum of one light failure every cave diving trip, these drills came in handy. They were, in a sense, life savers. Today, that sort of failure rate is not even close to the actual situation – lights rarely fail – but students in cave-diving courses still practice those skills. Probably always will because of our association with darkness and danger.

The dive community has enjoyed the benefits of innovations and technological master strokes in the past few years. The improvements in lighting must be close to the top of the list. A generation ago, dive lights, often bespoke designs from what were essentially garage operations, kicked out barely enough light to cast a shadow. These were susceptible to leaks, even dampness stopped them working, and battery life counted in minutes. Compared to what is available today, they seem as useful as a sharp stick would be to fend off a Velociraptor.

Halogen running off Nickel-Metal Hydride batteries, then LEDs coupled with Ni-lithium-based batteries have replaced lead-acid and tiny 40-WATT incandescent lamps purchased from the cave-diving section of The Home Depot or Canadian Tire. Specialized factory-made cave lights now produce thousands of lumens and last for hours. These have taken over completely, and now inexpensive alternatives, capable of flooding a cave the size of an NHL hockey rink, with enough light to satisfy a Bollywood director, are the norm.

To get an idea of how bright: Imagine you're driving at night when a luxury German sports car coming from the other direction doesn't bother to drop his headlights to low-beam, and you turn blind momentarily and the opening bars of *Set the Controls for the Heart of the Sun* blast from the car stereo. Well, that bright.

Incidentally, the 18650 Li-ion battery – the default power source for many cave lights today including the dill pickle-sized backup lights in many cave diver's kits – is also what powers a Tesla Model S! Not just one or two, which is all we use. More than 7,000 of them. Now, that's greedy. One hopes that they remember to leave a few for those of us exploring the dark reaches of mother nature.

Question Three

"WHAT'S A CAVE DIVER EXACTLY; WHO DOES THAT SILLINESS? IS THERE A SPECIAL CLASS? IS IT THE SAME AS A DIVE INSTRUCTOR?"

- These are questions non-divers, and even certified divers ask. The cheap and cheerful answers are:: It's complicated... and changing all the time; Yes, there are several classes involved; Definitely not the same, and don't come close to telling the whole story. You deserve better, so, here goes.

Some actors are brilliant at adopting regional accents for their roles on stage or in front of the camera. It looks and sounds easy to do: to sound American, when you're not, or like middle -European aristocracy when you actually grew up around the corner from Toronto's St. Lawrence Market. But of course, it isn't easy at all. It takes some talent and an ear for where to stress and relax the sounds you make. There's work and practice behind disguising something as ingrained as, say, the received pronunciation of a Winchester College graduate, and replace it with the short vowel confusion of a full-on Geordie accent or Appalachian Mountain Talk; or the reverse! But some can do it with gusto and produce amazingly accurate and totally convincing end-results.

A few don't have to. They are lucky enough to have a trademark way of talking that's super-glued to their character; Christopher Walken and Michael Caine come to mind. Others, less fortunate in a way, make an art of being a vocal chameleon.

I'm not sure what accent experts like Meryl Streep and Idris Elba, sound like at home, when they're not working on a "new" voice. You see, Elba was born in Hackney, at one-time a rough area of East London — now voted one of the city's most liveable boroughs, shockingly.

And a Hackney accent is pretty thick, but Elba is etched on my memory as Nelson Mandela, with that man's distinct South African clipped pronunciation included in the pantomime. And I can't even guess where Streep was from originally and what accent she grew up with. Perhaps she was always a mimic even as a kid, because her range covers a world of different sounds and adjustments in her speech cadence. She is truly masterful; an incredible talent who lives in the skin of her screen character; a true shapeshifter as well as a vocal acrobat. However, she will forever be telling me about dingoes and her baby, so is she Australian?

Then there's Gary Oldman. Is he Dracula, a spaceman arms dealer, an unhinged DEA agent, Batman's Commissioner Gordon, or George Smiley? He really is exceptional at faking accents; so good he needed a voice coach to relearn his natural New Cross/London

S.E.15/Millwall supporter's accent. He lost it somewhere in the space between roles, like loose change in the rec-room sofa, and needed help fishing for it between cushions.

In an actor's world, the ability to pull off that level of fakery, wins awards, but in real life... not so much. Most of us trying to fake an accent deeply enough to convince our audience sooner or later get totally caught in a net of disbelief. We may convince for a sentence or two, and we may pull off a reasonable stereotype for several paragraphs, but then reality kicks in and catches us out. Then we sound more like Muppets than magicians, and it ends in laughter. I'm told my attempt at Birmingham, for example, is several counties off with the Irish Sea between.

To be masterful, requires some talent. All that plus the guiding touch of an expert vocal coach; what amounts to training and instruction. Plus, a dumpster truck-full of practice. That's what makes the extraordinary look easy: talent, an appreciation that this is fun, an instructor who knows their stuff, and time to practice.

There are people like Oldman, Streep, and Elba making all sorts of other complex things look easy. Mountain biking, base jumping, white-water canoeing, rock climbing, even cave diving. But beware the multiple takes and seamless editing of YouTube. It's never as easy as it looks. High-risk activities (and all of those qualify) should carry the common-sense warning: Do not try this at home, you could get hurt, or worse.

So, answering the questions at the top of this chapter in a random order; yes, there is a special class. Cave divers are specialists who, because of quite intense training and specific experience, are several postal codes away from run of the mill divers. Just my opinion, which is a biased one perhaps.

Cave divers are experts with a passion for what they do and not to be confused with SCUBA divers generally; not even instructors who teach regular SCUBA diving programs. Open water Instructors (master instructors, even open water instructor trainers) learn how to teach beginners to dive. Their skills include herding cats and smiling in spite of it all. They have the great privilege of leading punters on brief visits to an alien world filled with strange, exotic creatures, where gravity can be tamed, and all this surface nonsense can be put into perspective. But none of that counts in a cave. Completely different rules, totally unrelated skills. Instructors – the regular kind – are not cave divers and don't belong in a cave.

Cave divers – the ones who stick at it and make it look easy – the ones who excel and glide and float suspended in the water column with quiet hands and feet, showing the same level of control in the water as a fish, who look solid and painted in place and like they belong where we find them, well they are the Oldmans and Streeps, and Elbas in the diving world. Actually, let me adjust that statement. Responsible cave divers, and certainly the generation of cave diving instructors who are working and teaching now, today, meet an even higher standard because they do what they do underwater, in the dark, a long way from a second, third or fourth take.

SCUBA DIVING

So, yes, there is a special class, but what does that mean? Let's start at the beginning. There is a general misunderstanding with at least half of the non-diving public (more than that, probably) that learning to SCUBA dive is monochrome umbrella rather than the multi-coloured circus tent that it is.

That misunderstanding supposes, once someone slaps on a pair of fins and learns to blow bubbles underwater, that's it. Folks who do this get some sort of a licence and they're done. Exactly what that <licence> is and what it covers and how that all works with the SCUBA police isn't clear, but the basic understanding is, it's a licence: a carte blanche. After that, there's nothing a diver can't do and nowhere they can't go. Any shipwreck, any cave, hundreds of metres deep for as long as they like. Dives on tropical reefs, under artic ice, in fresh water or the saltiest oceans, no problems. It's pretty much all the same. They pull on a wetsuit and off they go. They can do anything they like, and it is open season for cavaliers and cowboys. The only limits to what they can get up to are how crazy they are, how lucky they feel, and how their stars are aligned the day they go diving.

The reality is nothing like that at all.

It's fair to put the blame the SCUBA diving industry for doing a very shoddy public relations job explaining that there's more to the dive business than one colour and one size fits all. Let's see what we can do to fill in some blank spots.

When the couple living down the street travel to Malta during Easter break and come back flashing photos of their underwater diving experience – accomplished in an afternoon without leaving their resort – the obvious conclusion is to think of them as divers, but actually, they are not. Their one-day experience, which SCUBA certification agencies (and there are more than 120 of them globally) refer to by various names: Try Dive, Try Scuba,

Introduction to Scuba, Scuba Experience, and so on. These all boil down to a supervised dip in the ocean strapped into the bare minimum of dive kit, and just enough instruction to breathe underwater. This sort of happening, great as far as it goes and certainly a potentially memorable experience to add to everyone's I Love Me Wall, consists of a couple of hours looking at a flipchart by the pool followed by a few minutes in a shallow lagoon, wondering where the instructor is and if that dim shadow in the distance is a shark.

The whole thing is supposed to be a lark and, for a lucky few, starts them thinking, "SCUBA is fun and exciting, I want more!" The Try Dive experience is designed pretty much as the SCUBA equivalent of a gateway drug to hook punters into signing up for the real thing... a full-on entry-level SCUBA course.

These try dive events are an important marketing tool, and sometimes they work the way the agency intended. A surprising number of present-day industry professionals admit they got hooked on diving after doing a try dive or something similar. However, try dives themselves do not make big headlines at the dive agency and do not add numbers to the 1.7 million SCUBA diving certs reported annually.

To count in those numbers, one has to take the next step and earn an open water diver certification. That's the entry level to the diving "family", and, on a good day- with a responsible instructor taking their job seriously -about ten times more involved (more entertaining and more fun) than the pool/lagoon dip our friends in Malta lucked into.

Once again, there are around an astonishing 120 SCUBA diving agencies. This includes small regional outfits with a couple of dozen affiliated dive stores and a small cadre of instructors. Hardly surprising, and some of them are legacies from old-school outfits, youth clubs, associated sports clubs and generally are found in regions beyond the reach of the mainstream. For brevity's sake, we can ignore these and focus instead on what's called the Big Seven (BSAC, CMAS, NAUI, PADI, RAID, SDI, and SSI). These are the most active, globally recognised, paid up members of industry-wide standards organisations such as the WRSTC (World Recreational Scuba Training Council) and they carry other accreditations, too.

Each of these organisations has dive shops around the world flying their flag and hundreds, thousands, of instructors on their books. They are the backbone of the SCUBA industry and when people talk about being certified as a diver, chances are better than good it was through one of these seven agencies.

These agencies list courses following very similar criteria and adhere to very similar standards. There are some differences in how those standards are interpreted and enforced, but we'll get to that in a later chapter. What's relevant now is that since they follow similar guidelines, they each offer more or less equivalent courses. These are labelled differently for marketing purposes, but an open water diver with agency ABC is about the same as an autonomous diver with sister agency XYZ.

Essentially, the Big Seven have around six to ten core programs that follow on from a basic open water course. These courses build skills and introduce students to some of the more complex aspects of diving, dive gear, and different environments (night dives, diving a little deeper than the 20-metre limit for the basic certification and so on).

In addition to those, there are more than three dozen specialties that interweave and add more intrigue and depth to the core programs. So, now we're at more than 40 different courses available, and that's not counting the professional level courses (instructor and above) associated with each of those core programs and specialties.

Then there are technical diving programs to add to that list, and cave diving is a subset of that category. Technical diving covers a broad list of activities that include advanced training at considerable depth (as deep as 100 metres), staged decompression (very slow ascent from deep and long dives designed to mitigate the risk of decompression sickness... the bends), the use of breathing gases other than air, and working with special equipment (closed-circuit rebreathers for example).

According to DAN (Diver's Alert Network, a sort of industry watchdog, part research, part insurance company), there are fewer than 150,000 active technical divers in the world. The best guess is that two percent of those technical divers become cave divers. So, 1.7 million SCUBA certs a year, and at most, one in ten results in an active technical diver, and a fraction of those take up cave diving.

A recent survey by one of the agencies that offers cave training (and not all of them do), suggested there are fewer than 15,000 active cave divers at any time, globally. If SCUBA diving qualifies as a niche market, technical diving is a niche within that niche, and so on.

The best analogy I can muster is those Ukrainian nesting dolls, Matryoshka dolls, because cave diving is a niche within the technical diving niche, inside the SCUBA niche, which is nested inside a larger doll labelled "high-risk activities that people do for fun."

THE TYPICAL CAVE DIVER

And so, cave diving is absolutely well outside anyone's definition of mainstream. It requires specialised equipment, carries increased risk (and SCUBA is risky enough on its own), and takes a fun hobby to the borders of obsession.

DAN's statistics gurus weren't specific about definitions, but given the source, and diving morphology's current guidelines, a technical diver would have taken at least a handful of advanced diving courses well beyond the basic core programs. These would cover advanced and somewhat esoteric swimming and buoyancy skills, detailed diving physiology, understanding and application of gas laws (chemistry and biology 101), environmental concerns and respect for anything beneath to water's surface: wildlife, wrecks, artifacts, and so on. They will have also invested considerable amounts of time and money.

Cave diving is a step further down the rabbit hole than that.

So, who are they? From a sales and marketing point of view, they're an attractive demographic because, like anyone involved in an equipment-intensive pastime, they spend money. They spend on travel, training, and any piece of equipment in which they see value (a dive computer, an underwater scooter, cameras, lenses and waterproof housings, drysuits, but most definitely, spares of everything and anything). They are arch consumers in the most attractive and activity-centric way possible. And in their defence, any equipment that is going into a cave, must be as close to totally reliable as practical. A part of every pre-dive check is to make sure everything going into the dark looks, feels, and is functional. The worn, frayed, or iffy gets tossed and replaced.

Something that may seem odd, disingenuous even, when looking from the outside, is that the majority of these men and women are risk averse. Certainly, they get a thrill from visiting places that only a handful of humans have seen, and in some cases, going to places where no humans have been since the last ice age, when most of the caves now open to diving were dry. And they get satisfaction from the preparation and planning for something complex and compelling that carries a heavy personal responsibility.

For most, being in the cave offers a unique and powerful, totally Zen experience, if one wants it to be so. But taking unplanned for, unnecessary risks is not part of the package. At least for the sensible ones.

There is one other character trait to add to the generic profile of a someone who takes up diving in caves for fun; and while not necessary, is definitely a benefit. It is having an unflappable nature: being slow to excite, and able to deal with sudden surprises more practically, sensibly than most.

Robert White uses a wonderful scale to assess how well a person might take to the calmness and focus of meditation. In *Why Buddhist is True*, he puts the volatility of a kid who's apt to show his frustration by throwing a chicken wing at a dinner guest at one end, the Dali Lama at the other. While I have met plenty of cave divers who have all of the self-control of a kid throwing food or their toys out of the pram, universally, the way they deal with stress is weighted heavily towards his Holiness' end of the spectrum. The average cave diver is better able to deal with the unexpected with an "Oh, well, that's interesting... let's fix it..." attitude rather than an "Oh my gawd! Now, what do I do?" freeze, flight, fawn, or fight approach.

Besides that, there is a generational thing to consider. The cliche, especially in SCUBA diving, is that the current generation don't get it, they've had it easy, and went from zero to hero in a weekend.

THIS IS THE BEST GENERATION

Here's where the "when we were youngsters, we walked uphill to school, both ways, in the sleet, heels being nipped by wolves, carrying a full-sized oak desk on our backs, and we lived in a shoebox" syndrome shows its face. I feel the opposite is true. The current line-up of young cave pros are better examples of how dive professionals should act, and are more serious about refining their craft than the past generation ever were.

Mine is a contentious opinion, but it seems a valid assessment applied to North Florida and Mexico's Yucatan Peninsula. I've been watching changes happen in those two distinct and very different communities for four decades. Changes were needed. Thirty years ago, cave diving in north Florida was as near to a closed shop as possible; with the door as tightly guarded against newcomers as a mediaeval craftsman's guildhall.

Perhaps cave instructors and divers wanted to be added to the list of protected occupations: masons, marblers, coopers, thatchers, and so on. It was, in Florida, mostly an old boys' club, with a dash of redneck, grits and moonshine thrown in for good measure;

on reflection, quite a crazy ride, but neither progressive nor inclusive.

Inevitably, change came with a new generation who enjoy and project a more open, realistic perspective. The cave community is where it is today by standing on what Sir Issac Newton called the shoulders of giants: England's Cave Diving Group, Sheck Exley, Tom Mount, Larry Green, Hal Watts et al in Florida, and a long list of men and women around the world who pushed limits, often by seat-of-the-pants trial and error, and opened up a new world for those who followed. But hindsight throws a harsh light on everything it touches; some of those giants in the cave world had clay-like feet.

As a group, the generation of cave specialists and instructors teaching now pay more attention to keeping their skills sharp, staying in shape, respecting the environment, building positive landowner relationships, engaging in responsible exploration, and delivering the best, most thorough training to their students.

They also question the status quo. They ask why things are done that way when this way works better. They suggest change, then demonstrate its effectiveness. And all of that invites creativity... and progress. In one of his excellent essays, American Jacob M. Appel wrote that the most dangerous ideas are not those that challenge the status quo but those so embedded in the status quo, so wrapped in a cloud of inevitability, that we forget they are ideas at all. Good words to judge progress by.

All in all, now is a good time to learn to cave dive.

Of course, all this is just the opinion of one of those old guys who used to hang tetra-paks of pina colada six metres deep on the way into the cave to drink during long decompression stops on the way out. So, take that into consideration.

And, the final answer to this chapters questions, don't worry if you forget all of the above. There's truth in the standing joke that warns not to worry too much about recognizing a cave diver and finding out what they do. You don't need to sweat it. Sooner or later, they'll let you know.

Question Four

HOW COME YOU DON'T GET LOST... ARE THERE SIGNPOSTS AND STUFF?

- If ever you make a presentation to Kids about diving
of any sort, but certainly cave diving, they ask these
questions without fail.

It would be silly to pretend that people don't get lost inside caves. Sometimes, they do. Occasionally someone messes up and doesn't make it out until someone else goes in to fetch them. This is usually some poor soul who is part of a local volunteer group dedicated to diver recovery (rarely rescue). But those unfortunate cases really are exceptions. Cave diving is dangerous, but if one follows the rules, not as dangerous as all that. Honestly.

The first of those rules applies to all types of SCUBA diving and it is: don't hold your breath. Nasty things can happen if a diver holds their breath, especially while ascending because the compressed gas in their lungs expands as the water pressure around them drops, and their lungs over expand and tear.

The easy solution is don't hold your breath.

The second rule follows on from that and is: always have something to breathe so there's no temptation to hold your breath. This is a very important rule for every diver but especially so for those inside a cave. For someone in the ocean, fresh air is overhead and perhaps 30 or 40 metres away. For a cave diver, fresh air may be an hour's swim and more than a kilometer away.

Related to both of those, and yet another piece of advice particularly appropriate for cave divers and the questions above is: don't get lost. Wayland Rhys Morgan said "Without Jesus in my life, I'm told my soul is lost. I'm not at all sure I have a pony in that race, but I do know without a piece of string to follow coming out of a cave, my life is lost."

As outlandish as it sounds, not getting lost in a cave is all about following a piece of string.

ARIADNE'S RED WOOL

I have no idea who originally thought of using string as a guideline to find the way into a cave, and back out again. It may have been some brave pioneer walking into a hole in England's Cheddar Gorge, or Abe Davis who is credited with being the first person to explore a cave in North Florida. In fact, it was probably an early art critic on their way in to see the latest ochre and charcoal rendering on the walls of Altamira. However, I like imagining that some early cave-diving pioneer was a big fan of Greek mythology. Particularly the story about Ariadne, Theseus, and the Minotaur.

The short version of that story is that the Minotaur – an enormous monster, part man, part fighting bull – had overstayed whatever welcome it had and needed to be done away with. A warrior called Theseus volunteered to get the job done. A nasty complication was that the Minotaur wasn't just ultra-mean, extremely strong, and with an appetite for snacking on people. He also lived in the center of a huge labyrinth; a maze of tunnels so vast and complex, that once inside, it was impossible to find one's way back out. If you have nightmares about getting lost in a strange city without cell service – so no access to Google Maps or Waze – and a looming deadline for an important meeting with an old workmate, an art-director you haven't seen in years, perhaps you have empathy.

But enter the hero – or in this case, the heroine – Ariadne. She was smart enough not to go into the labyrinth herself. However, she did weave a long red string made from wool, and she shared this with the warrior Theseus and sent him in.

Ariadne held one end and waited for him at the entrance to the labyrinth. He held the other end and went inside searching for the monster.

There are several versions of the story – Greek myths usually have regional variations – but at the core of all of them is that Theseus slew the Minotaur and followed the thread back out to the open. What happens after that varies. One version paints a very poor picture of Theseus, but no matter. The lesson for us is that a piece of string (red wool or otherwise) is the proven hero/heroine-tested solution for finding your way around in a maze.

And that's the trick that cave divers borrow from ancient Greece and Ariadne.

Way back in 1979, a guy called Sheck Exley wrote a small but influential booklet titled: *Basic cave diving: a blueprint for survival.* We're told never to judge a book by its cover, and in this case, that's sound advice. *Blueprint* is not an impressive thing to look at.

At first glance it has all the presence of something a primary school teacher would share with their class in those days before laptop computers, word processing programs, and the internet. (Perhaps an interesting side note is that Exley was in fact a high-school maths teacher besides being a cave-diving guru.)

Anyway, his book's layout is amateurish, and the typesetting is an awkward reminder of the stuff kicked out by the IBM Selectric typewriter I learned to type on in the 1960s. However, it is the closest thing the cave-diving community has to a holy writ. The information and advice it contains, remain the gold standard.

To put it into perspective, it was published at a time when there was little in the way of structured and sanctioned instruction to teach cave diving techniques. At the time, cave-diving itself was a moving target and still very definitely "in flux." Mainstream SCUBA agencies wouldn't touch anything remotely technical – including nitrox[1]- let alone diving in a water-filled hole in solid limestone. Even finding someone to teach you a cave-diving class was akin to linking up with the local village wizard who was willing to share the secrets of the black arts. It was like being involved in some middle-English

---

[1] A mix of nitrogen and oxygen similar to air but with a higher percentage of oxygen. Once decried as highly dangerous for recreational SCUBA divers by several of the mainstream agencies but now in common use.

fantasy novel; not quite a search for the Holy Grail, but definitely, cave-diver training was a freakish curiosity outside of a handful of small, close-knit sump-diving communities in the West of England, or a select group of highly selective experts in North Florida's clear-springs karst country.

Directly related perhaps to that lack of appropriate training and dim general awareness of its value, this was also during a period when there were an alarming number of dive fatalities, especially in the Florida caves, where Exley lived and worked. It was this series of tragedies that triggered Exley to publish his little booklet.

Basic cave diving: a blueprint for survival contains a list of best practices, suggested rules, and things NOT to do. Exley included – as an introduction to each chapter – examples of real incidents in which divers had broken 'the rules' and perished. He wrote that since he had logged more than 2,000 cave dives at the time of writing, the pieces of advice he was sharing were "not based on mere theory and conjecture: they have been proven repeatedly in actual field conditions, and they work."

Interesting perhaps is that to this day, the majority of classes preparing divers for cave diving include a learning module on accident analysis; essentially what Exley opened every chapter of his little manual more than 50 years ago, and although a lot of time has passed since he wrote "Blueprint" and in that time many, many things to do with technical diving and cave diving in particular have radically changed, Exley's list is as valid now as it ever was.

In chapter one, he deals with some basic navigation issues. Exley's first rule for survival is stated in the first couple of paragraphs. It is to "always use a single, continuous guideline from the entrance of the cave throughout the dive." Ariadne's red wool.

In most explored caves, AKA tourist caves[2], there is a permanent guideline, usually installed and maintained by local cave instructors and volunteer cave divers. This line is a lifeline. As long as a diver can see or feel it and, provided they can 'read' the instructions it gives them, they should know where they are in the cave, and, critically, which way is out.

Today, in in Florida, Mexico, the Caribbean, France and most of Europe, these permanent lines are nylon kernmantle (more durable than wool).

Kernmantle is a tough, specialized cord with a core of several twisted lines protected by a braided sheath. Depending on the environment (things such as flow and the size and layout of the cave's main passage, where the line sits, and the 'traffic' the cave attracts), this permanent guideline would optimally be between 4mm and 6mm thick. It's usually white – or a light yellow labelled Golden Rod – but key to its function is that it is secured well, is robust enough to resist fraying, is easy to see, and is installed in a way that allows divers to pass without getting tangled in it.

Also, this permanent line is a visual reference and NOT a sort of rock-climbing aid: that is, it can't be be pulled or tugged on because it will certainly break or come away in your hand.

---

[2] Tourist caves in not a pejorative term and isn't intended to trivialize the skills or experience needed to visit one cave as opposed to another. It simply describes a cave popular as a dive site and often visited, which also has well-maintained permanent lines in place.

Again, in most explored caves, it's common practice for the permanent line to start a few minutes swim into the cave rather than beginning in open water. This is to discourage open water divers from seeing a "piece of string" and following it to see where it leads or messing with it and dislodging it.

This means, that on their way into the cave, divers install their own, temporary line from outside the cave's dripline (the point where the overhead begins and where one could shelter from pouring rain – theoretically). That temporary line winds carefully through the cavern and connects with the installed permanent line where it begins. And thus, the diver and her mates have a continuous guideline to the exit... a known exit... the way they came in.

LINEMARKERS... SIGNPOSTS ALONG THE STRING ROAD

Following a length of nylon kernmantle to find the way around in a cave sounds simple, and it would be a straightforward exercise if caves were like drainpipes. One way in, turn around, one way out.

But that's not the case. Caves, notably highly decorated ones with speleothems hanging from ceiling to floor and massive flowstones blocking passages, are not like drainpipes. Even the phreatic ones that have never been dry and therefore are not decorated and are the closest thing to a pipeline, even those have side passages and confusing twists and turns.

Sedimentary rock is not deposited in a uniform slab like a screed of concrete. Every generation of tiny creatures whose calcium "shells" build one upon another lived under different stresses and conditions. They had challenges or advantages when they were alive and growing millions of years ago, and that resulted in them leaving layers with a variety of thickness: a different position relative to its neighbours, and subtle changes in which species of tiny sea creatures were dominant. As a result, the rock's density varies and so it dissolves following an irregular pattern; completely randomly in fact.

The result is a complex, almost fractally shaped, three-dimensional matrix, that we call a cave – a negative space rather like a rest in a piece of music singing the song of its creation millions of years in the past. Its shape tells the story of acidic rain-water's slow journey from falling on the jungle floor and seeping through rock to the water table deep underground. In effect, the shape of a cave follows gravity's relentless attraction on water over time. Which, when one considers the situation creatively, makes it a four-dimensional historic structure. Pure alien architecture.

Antoni Gaudí surely visited caves before imagining La Sagrada Família, Barcelona's mind-bending but as yet unfinished cathedral.

Beyond Gothic, beyond Catalan Modernism, just the Hall of the Mountain King scaled up to enormous size and dimensions, mineral but organic, going on and on endlessly... and easy to get lost in but for string and the strange plastic signposts cave divers have adopted to follow.

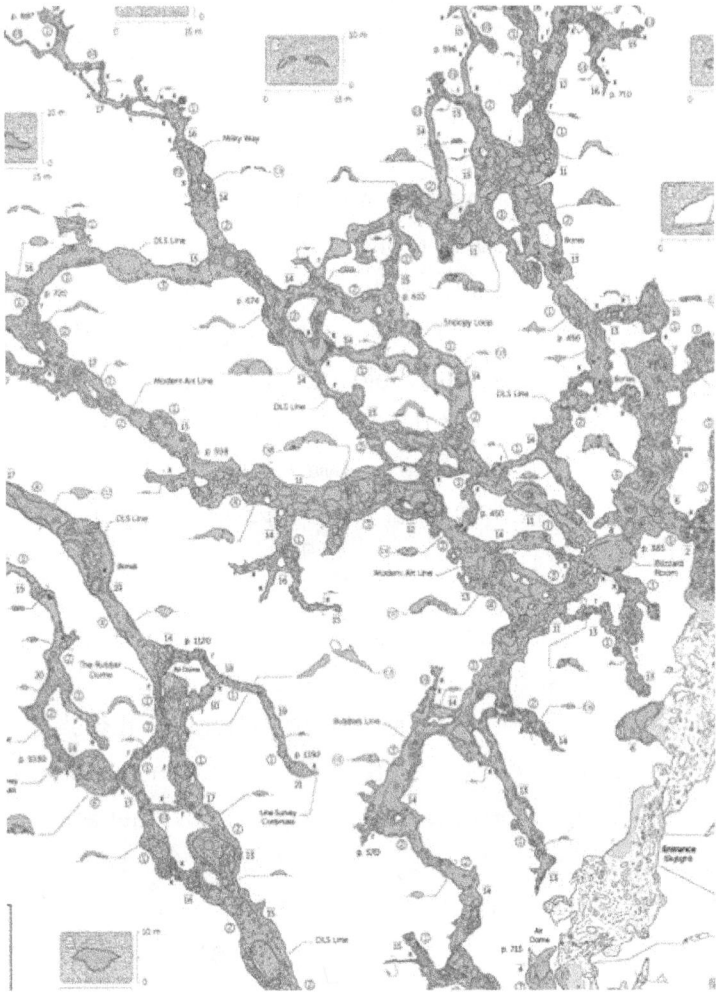

SECTION OF TYPICAL MEXICAN CAVE SYSTEM'S MAP

As mentioned already to save W. R. Morgan's life in a cave, neither string nor Jesus is enough. (Just look at the map above, to see how complex an afternoon swim in a cave can be.) There has to be a way to show him and other cave divers, which way is in and which way out. Which one - in a confusion of pathways - is the one that leads to a known destination and safety, and which one leads to a very bad day at the office? And yes, there are signposts doing this job. They are small pieces of plastic just a few sizes up from a fancy pictorial postage stamp. There are three basic designs each intended for a specific purpose, and collectively they're called line markers.

Directional line markers are an acute isosceles triangle, similar to an arrowhead; non-directional cookies are basically round like a small biscuit or cookie; hybrid or REM (Reference Exit Markers) are rectangular with one end blank like a tiny slate. All three have offset notches to make it possible and simple to attach them to the guideline. (Note for fans of the 1980s Athens, GA-based rock band, the line marker is pronounced as a word almost like "rim" but with an "e" in place of the "i", rather than "R.E.M." but with a totally different meaning.)

There's no need to bother with a full description of how they are used, but the little arrowheads are the only type of line marker installed on a cave's permanent line; usually. Since there's currently no universally agreed code, there is some allowance or slop in what is and what is not done in each region. Even how they are used from system to system in the same region. However, the sharp point of the triangle-shaped ones ALWAYS point to the end of the line. It'd be wrong to say or think that they point to the exit, because since the line intentionally ends short of the cave's actual exit, end of the line is more accurate than calling it an exit because that is what they reference.

Cookies or non-directional markers are team-specific and are used as an attendance marker: a "we came this way" breadcrumb that everyone in a dive team understands and agrees upon. There's some variation with these line markers too, especially since the appearance of 3-D printers, and individuals take every liberty possible regarding colour, shape, and size. But that's okay because these being team specific mean if one sees a cookie on the line and it is NOT one of yours or your buddy teams' it's ignored.

REMs or hybrid line markers are individual-specific. Other members of the folks you're diving with have to be made aware of them (what they look like, how they are marked to personalize them, what colour and size they are, and so on), but they are intended as a personal breadcrumb, waypoint, or reminder.

They're designed asymmetrically with a small blank space at one end. This is the "slate" and can carry a message to "self" or can be left blank. A typical tactic is to pre-mark a bunch of REMs with times, distances, or survey marks, and attach them on the line at appropriate spots. You certainly let your buddies know you are placing them, but they are for you... a kind of reassurance on the way in, and certainly comforting on the way out, especially in an unfamiliar cave.

The slate – the asymmetrical blank space at one end of the rectangular body of a REM – must always point back to the entrance, hence the 'hybrid' label since REMs can serve as a directional or a non-directional marker. They are very popular in Mexico where cave topography is generally much more complex compared to, say, North Florida.

A political note, I'm not sure what the history is with the late Bil Phillips (the REM's inventor) and the Florida cave-diving community, but there are cave people there in the Sunshine State who are anything but sunny about REMs, and who swear that just carrying them about your person is as close to a crime against reason and common sense as one can get.

It's bizarre because Bil Phillips was one of the most non-confrontational, laid back, late vintage Canadian hippies in diving, and his little plastic travel-aides do a stellar job as mini-signposts. Which proves you cannot please everyone and so it goes.

Question Five

HOW DANGEROUS IS CAVE DIVING?

- "Not dangerous at all, mum... don't worry about me."
The author speaking to Joyce Amelia Thrower in the
early years of the 1990s.

Niccolo Machiavelli gets a bum rap in my opinion. His best-known work, Il Principe (The Prince), is a detailed warning about the dark side of human nature, the duplicity of politics, the pratfalls of acquiring power, and how easily disconnected from humanity a person can become. That may sound like a current story, but *The Prince* is an allegory from 16th-century Italy which, sadly, still rings true today. At that time in the 1500s, Florence - the city at the centre of Machiavelli's story - was ground zero for everything corrupt and villainous in a political state, and Machiavelli took on the task of pointing out the lunacy of it all. Yet, we've added "Machiavellian" to our language as a synonym for cunning, and bad faith; of using new-speak and fake news to bend opinion, and deep lies told to cover guilt. It is as though he wrote to promote the crass behaviour he satirised: as though he himself were the devil.

He didn't; he isn't. Thinking otherwise is missing the point. *The Prince* was intended as a very clever put down of the Medici family – who ruled Florence – and their omnibus of rottenness. He wasn't promoting bad behaviour or writing a how-to for 21st century politicians, he was issuing a warning.

But regardless, even if you disagree with this interpretation of the book and are happy with what on that basis end up as twisted back-to-front, inside-out contributions to our language, you must admit, his writing is masterful.

Machiavelli gave us much to think about. I particularly like his eccentric and pertinent viewpoint on danger: *Never was anything great achieved without it*. I think he meant that without satire or renaissance tongue-in-cheek. If the practice of hanging heraldry above our front doors was still a thing, that would make a splendid family motto.

What's missing though – and another general misunderstanding of the man's central premise – is that while he does not define danger far beyond the possibility of being stabbed in the back by an underling, he does tell us there's a world of difference between living with danger and taking unjustified risks.

For example, knowing when there is a crowd of sycophants waiting in the alleyway – each carrying a sword on his belt – prudence requires taking a different route to supper,

But back to the question at hand. Notwithstanding the white lie I told my mum when I started cave diving, it is dangerous. As I write this, a guy called Edd Sorenson has just pulled another poor dead soul out of a restriction at Jackson Blue Springs. That's a cave in Marianna, Florida, USA, near to where Edd and his wife Stacey live and own a dive operation.

Unfortunately, this was not the first and will not be the last person to die cave diving. But then, no foul, people die walking to Tim Hortons to pick up donuts and coffee. They die driving to the office, and they die sitting with the cat on their lap watching comedy special reruns on HBO. It's about perspective. To paraphrase Niccolo, everything great (or fun) always comes with some sort of danger attached.

Take the perfect breakfast of Ben & Jerry's ice cream, a can of Brio, and a robust cup of Italian coffee for example. I'm told that's dangerous. As mentioned, it's about perspective.

So, let's start by establishing that although people do die in caves, very few of those incidents can really be classified as true accidents. Too many are the result of simple and totally unnecessary errors of judgement and systemic oversights. These - coupled with misunderstandings and misinterpretations of what's going on - lead to total breakdowns of logic and the application of inappropriate responses to system failures. People screw up. But those are not accidents; they are consequences.

The cop-out reaction is to say all that grief and mayhem adds up to human error. But to arrive at a clear understanding of what that means, and perhaps how to make it stop or at very least avoid personal involvement, one needs to know which human and which error.

For example, was the oversight handed to the victim through poor training and poor reinforcement of limits post-training? Or was the issue raised because of a community bias encouraging myopic thinking and taking shortcuts? Or is there something more basic at play?

There is advice printed on the certification cards every diver gets when they graduate from any level of training. It warns that the holder is 'qualified to dive in conditions similar to or better than those encountered during training'. However, human nature drives innovative departures from best practice.

In real life, SCUBA divers routinely ignore those guidelines and go beyond the limits set out on those cards very soon after being handed them by their instructor.

For example, it is not unusual to find scads of open water divers (beginners with four dives logged and nothing more) dropping to 30 metres or beyond at some point during their first dive trip. Their suggested maximum depth is 20 metres or less (10 metres shallower), but they do it anyway. The dive community is sloppy at enforcing limits, and unremittingly lax at setting hard boundaries. (Or explaining convincingly why those limits and boundaries are there in the first place.)

A significant number of fatalities in caves – just as for fatalities in every high-risk activity including diving of every kind – involve people exceeding the training they've had, and not sheltering within the limits of whatever recent experience they have gained since that training. To a casual onlooker, their behaviour may seem like they're just willfully avoiding good advice. But, while that's a simple answer, what's at play is human nature.

To understand that fully, we have to be mindful of our natural inclination to push limits and act differently to what we know is the norm, safe, and established. It's acceptable to the hive, then, that instead of doing what's right and what's normal, people decide instead to do something different; something they know is a shortcut and riskier but is worth trying anyway because "rules are there to be tested".

Take Ontario's Hwy 400 close to my home. When the speed limit was raised recently from 100 kilometers an hour to 110, the average speed increased from around 110 kph, to more than 125. The logic being that the police patrolling that road with speed gun in hand, will not bother to hand out tickets to drivers doing "just a few clicks over the limit". Nothing in that logic acknowledges the condition of the road (unchanged), the capacity of a car's braking system (unchanged), or that increased speed requires better driver attention and reaction time. This means a fair number of the drivers passing by Parry Sound are happy to ignore limits as long as they don't get a speeding ticket. That's human nature.

For tens of thousands of years, our early ancestors resisted change and turned away from new ideas. The patterns and techniques they used to make stone tools stayed unchanged for hundreds of generations. But something dramatic changed all that. Perhaps a few additional grams of brain matter dumped in an ancestor's skull, or an extra fold in their frontal lobe turned on a creative, defiant gene. Whatever it was – overnight in evolutionary terms – that individual's descendants went from using weapons of wood and napped flint to designing missile guidance systems.

We get into trouble because we think we're smarter than the status quo and we love to break rules. A generation ago we taught kids that the ability to use tools is what sets us apart from every other animal on earth. That's not true. Crows use tools, so do ants. Chimps use tools, so do tuskfish and octopuses.

What sets us apart is that we like to cheat, and we'll do so at regular intervals if we think we can get away with it. Hence dicey behaviour, unorthodoxy, creativity, and for the unfortunate, the so-called accidents that follow. In every activity, from wonky bricklaying and botched thoracic surgery to dodgy cave diving, our fellow humans have a long history of breaking the rules of the game, or making up new ones as we play.

FIVE TYPES OF VICTIMS

But it's not just breaking the rules alone that causes things to go terribly wrong. That simply puts some poor punter at increased risk, and risk is fickle. It will sit with its arms folded doing nothing before it moves a muscle or blinks. We can tempt it to react again and again and get away with it. But when it's the most inconvenient and least expected, risk will make one move and the whole world will tumble like the wooden blocks in a game of Jenga.

So, it's about breaking the rules and getting away with it. Getting away with it until things change and the unholy alliance of circumstances that lead to a cul-de-sac ending in catastrophe.

While preparing notes to answer this question with more honesty than I shared with my mother, I realised that cave fatalities can be grouped into five pretty obvious categories, each with one major flaw that weakens any resistance to chaos.

The first are students who are actually on a course and under supervision of a certified cave instructor. These incidents are as rare as diamond icebergs floating on a sea of liquid gold. I know of only one.

The second are brand new cave divers. These are the punters with their newly minted cave diver card in hand, who decide this whole cave diving thing is easier than people make it out to be. They decide to try a double stage dive to the back of beyond first time out. This is the Dunning-Kruger Effect in action. More common than category number one, but rare-ish.

Next are very experienced cave divers. These folks have the chops, required skills and kit, to know their way around risk. However, complacency creeps into their planning or execution, or their evaluation of their physical fitness. They may get away with being sloppy a dozen times or more, but at some point, something nasty hits the fan. Their experience can help them recover, but not always. The example here is the Normalisation of Deviance. More common than it should be and too often the result of a dogged refusal to make allowances for the inevitability of aging.

Then we have explorers. Explorers occasionally end their careers as statistics, but a totally different set of statistics to any of the four mistakes and surprises listed above.

There are several individuals and incidents to be put into this category, most recently a friend called Brett Hemphill. Brett, founder of a non-profit called Karst Underwater Research, died while surveying Phantom Springs, a deep cave system in Texas.

Brett knew the risks he worked under were multiplied by the nature of the cave and the depth he was at (considerably deeper than any dive agency sanctions), but he was comfortable being out there on a distant limb. He had considerable experience, plus the mental wherewithal to weigh those risks against the results he got.

However, he joins a disturbingly long list of friends to whom I no longer send Christmas cards. Somehow the tapped cliche "they died doing what they loved" falls a long way short of unpacking the reality of their passing.

The fifth and final victims are interlopers. These are the unfortunates who venture into caverns and caves without training, not carrying the required gear, and without knowing how little mercy an overhead environment shows the unprepared. This category is the most difficult to reconcile. This is the category that saddens me the most. Unnecessary, unfathomable, and considerably more horrific than most misadventures. More common than it should be, and a surprisingly large percentage of fatalities that happen in a cave, belong here. And we'll leave it at that.

IT'S ALL ABOUT PANIC... THAT'S THE SECRET

While it's instructive to know all of that, the cave diving community's duty is to come up with solutions. In a recent online article, one of the management team at RAID (one of the Big Seven dive agencies) explained that rather than a single major catastrophe, it's often the domino effect of a series of small emergencies that trigger a failure to thrive in a cave. Chris Haslem, who runs the agency's operations in part of Asia where there are extensive caves, said: "The most common emergencies for cave divers are small equipment issues, like torches flooding, reels tangling, mask-straps breaking, or minor navigational problems: all contingencies that can be managed with proper training, keeping calm, and a team ethos"

It's hard to fathom that one small inconvenience has enough power to bring down all that training, practice, and experience, but it happens. Explaining why exactly is less straightforward.

Panic is an uncontrolled, often irrational fear, shorting out the thinking part of a person's brain; the whole front-end of it. Millions of years of slow evolution and growth, and a lifetime of education and deliberate thought, adds up to naught in these cases.

Each of us has special triggers: a spider, a mouse, a zombie grabbing our arm in the dark. And unfortunately, for some, it's something trivial such as a mask strap breaking or a regulator first-stage suddenly giving up the ghost and starting to leak. Both of which are things they had been trained to respond and manage appropriately and without fuss or the distraction of panic.

But we should note that what is at play here has nothing to do with a panic disorder. Suffering from that would surely prevent anyone from venture into a cave in the first place and probably would make for a not very happy SCUBA diver of any description. (This references the self-policing aspect of the sport.)

CONTROL YOUR BREATH AND YOU CONTROL PANIC

This is situational panic. Allowing oneself to be squeezed out of a comfortable spot and into blankness: into a place where there is nothing but a threat. This particular road dead-ends in a place where the only possibilities on offer seem to be flight, fight, faun, or freeze. At every moment during a cave dive, none of those options will work. Flight is useless since running away from oneself doesn't work;

there's nothing to fight, unless you believe in Aluxes[3] and Trolls; a cave is indifferent to pleas for mercy and falling on one's knees and begging, and certainly, staying put, not moving, hoping everything can sort itself out, will not end well.

But panic and being squeezed out of your comfortable spot can be controlled.

The textbook suggestion for any diver faced with this situation – or preferably the situation a handful of nanoseconds before this situation – is to stop, think, act.

Although this sounds awfully simplistic, it's the best general advice to give. Stop for a moment and think about the situation. The most important thing is to understand priorities.

First is having something to beath. You could take the time to learn differential calculus or a few words of classical Greek underwater as long as there's something to breath. So, sorting out the gas supply is key. If that's secure, one has time to work out a righteous solution... or at least something that'll get you back to the surface bruised and sore perhaps, but intact and wiser.

Chances are if you've followed the rules or even travelled a little beyond them to push the edge of one's personal comfort zone, you'll come up with a workable solution for whatever's gone pear-shaped. Don't act until you have a plan. It may take a second, but it is the correct thing to do. Always.

---

[3] Alexes are part of Mayan mythology and are naughty spirits who protect the Cenotes.

One other thing. In panic mode, breathing is shallow and rapid, which on SCUBA (or a rebreather) is the worst thing possible. Instead, breathe deeply and slowly.

Slow down and breathe in as slowly, deeply, and as gently as possible. Breathe out slowly, deeply, and gently as possible. Keep this up until breathing returns to something resembling normalcy.

Some people find it helpful to count steadily from one to five on each inhalation and exhalation. And for a few cycles, they keep their eyes closed and focus on breathing and nothing else.

Another option is to use step-breathing to get things back under control. Of all the breathing techniques, this is the simplest to remember and safest to practice underwater on SCUBA since there is zero breath-holding involved.

Start by finding a stable spot. It's not a good idea to hold on to anything underwater except yourself, so do that or hold onto a buddy. Now breathe in for four seconds, brief pause, breathe out for four seconds. Then breathe in for five seconds, brief pause, and breathe out for five seconds. Finally breathe in for six seconds, pause, and out for six seconds. Do this three times. At the end of three cycles, everything should be under control. If not, repeat.

Another trick to slow the mind rampaging around like a monkey at the carnival is called 3-3-3 Focus. Think of three objects nearby and focus on them each for three seconds, then three sounds (same deal), and finally move three body parts, hands, feet, head, whatever. Repeat as required!

The final answer: the honest answer to my mother's question of course would have been: "I can't lie, it's dangerous, mum". And although none of this was intended to change anyone's mind about the risks and dangers present for cave divers, the hope is it has helped to point out that a critical part of the art of cave diving is to work at mitigating every possible risk and quelling, to the full extent of what's practical, the associated danger.

Question Six

HOW FAR CAN YOU GO?

- Almost everyone asks this because for most of us, the thought of swimming into a hole for a kilometer or more is unsettling. Mind-boggling. Jaw-dropping. So, people are justified to wonder how on earth does someone go further than a few body lengths and they wonder how going deeper is doable. The follow-up or directly related question to this is the ubiquitous: how long does your oxygen tank last?

Let's clear up a huge misunderstanding right here, right now. Except under special circumstances, which will be explained in a moment, SCUBA divers do not carry tanks of oxygen in the water; and certainly, do not dive with them.

What divers usually breathe is compressed air (regular air about 21 percent oxygen and 79 percent nitrogen); or Nitrox (a diving gas that contains an extra 'squirt' of oxygen compared to air);

or trimix (a blend of helium, oxygen, and nitrogen specifically for deeper diving to help manage narcosis and particularly gas density, which helps to lessen the work of breathing at depth).

Pure oxygen is used as a special gas to optimise decompression after long or deep dives: dives well beyond recreational limits and into the realm of technical diving. However, there is a hard limit on how deep 100 percent oxygen can be used: six metres or 20 feet and that's it! Any deeper than that, and the diver runs an elevated risk of experiencing a nasty reaction: a tonic-clonic seizure, which is not a happy experience at any time, particularly underwater.

So, the correct answer to how long does an oxygen tank last goes something like: Well, the generally accepted protocol is that the volume of oxygen in the tank is around two times that required by each diver to complete her planned decompression stops at six and three metres combined.

(A very quick note to explain decompression stops. When a diver breathes compressed gas of any kind at depth, their body absorbs gas, in particular the inert gas in what they have in their cylinders. Usually this would be nitrogen – a major component of our atmosphere – or nitrogen and helium – this is trimix and used in gases blended for deeper dives. To safeguard their health and well-being, as the diver travels back to the surface, they must make a slow, controlled ascent to allow their body to get rid of that absorbed gas. The diving world calls this slow journey back to fresh air, decompression, deco, or a decompression ascent. The variables considered in calculating the speed at which that absorbed gas is eliminated, are collectively part of decompression theory, and that, dear reader, is the topic for a doctoral thesis. Most divers rely on a dive computer to do the mathematics required to keep them safe.)

But that's a little too much information for most folks, so we just leave it at: we don't breathe oxygen. On the whole, it's easier, certainly more straightforward to say that than to watch someone's eyes glaze over when you prattle off all of the above.

Now, given a diver is breathing something more appropriate for her dive, let's try to deal with the <How Far> question. And before we start on details, there is the whiff of the: how long is a piece of string? about this question. It depends on so many variables.

When divers plan a cave dive, they usually have some sort of goal in mind. That may be to visit a particular area: the Swiss Siphon at Jailhouse Cenote for example (a particularly photogenic area of a popular Mexican cave). Or there may be a particular piece of kit or skill they want to try; or they may be setting up a circuit dive (Peacock to Orange Grove perhaps). Or they might want to carry full tanks of gas into the cave and leave them (stage them) for a big dive planned for a day or two into the future. Or they may be exploring a new section of cave, and the goal is to lay new line and come back with that new section surveyed as part of a planned mapping project. And of course, it might just be a dive whose plan is to relax and have fun. There are many variables at play here, and to be fair and to give a meaningful answer, we have to define a few boundaries and restrictions.

The first consideration always is NOT running out of something wholesome to breathe.

Since humans do poorly breathing water, fresh or salt, everything takes second place to gas management. True, there are protocols to share 'air' with a buddy – another dive-team member – if things go astonishingly pear-shaped. In open water, one can swim to the surface while doing this air sharing trick because the surface is a few metres directly overhead. This is what used to be taught as the primary solution to running out of air in a beginner's SCUBA course and it can work. There are better options, including proper gas management and situational awareness; the newer options to keep beginners save. Certainly, there are better options in a cave, because directly overhead is solid rock. Bolting for the surface is not one of them. And although there are techniques for sharing gas with a buddy if one runs low on gas in a cave, barring the intervention of the seven demons of hell or some other total catastrophe, getting into a situation where one needs to share air, is heavily frowned upon. There are very few Mulligans in cave diving.

The first line of defense against running out of gas is simple: cave divers follow a tight dive plan (very little if anything is left to chance), and they carry lots of spare gas. Helping to pad out their safety cushion a little more, they have a redundant gas source (at least two regulator systems) and plan very carefully how long their gas will last and how far they can travel using just a portion of that gas. All this is done long before they venture into the water. In short, they plan the dive thoroughly and stick to that plan.

To keep it simple, we'll look at the details such as the volume of breathing gas a diver can carry and how much they consume every minute they're diving, in Question Thirteen. Right now, we can satisfy curiosity and answer the question with a working guesstimate, using the basic guideline cave divers use to manage gas.

This guideline is the Rule of Thirds. If you're an artist or photographer, ignore what you're thinking. This rule has nothing to do with composition, creating a pleasing picture, or doing what artistic convention and art teachers around the world tell us to do.

The gas management version of the Rule of Thirds suggests using one-third of the starting volume of the compressed gas in the diver's tanks to swim into the cave, a second third to swim out, and the remaining third as contingency gas. I'm oversimplifying this a little, but you get the picture.

To translate this to real-world numbers, let's deal with divers who are using 11-litre aluminum cylinders (AKA aluminum 80s). This is a reasonable starting point given that this is the most common SCUBA cylinder, and available in most dive spots around the world. If a diver starts out with a pressure gauge attached to their tanks (and there will be two at least), showing 210 bar[4], they'll swim into the cave until that gauge reads 140 bar. At this point, they will have consumed 70 bar of gas, which is one-third of the 210 bar they began with. Put another way, at this point, our diver would have consumed roughly 1,500 litres of the approximately 4,600 litres of gas they started with. This, then, is a major waypoint on their dive and it's the point at which they will turn the dive around and start to swim out. During the return journey, if everything goes as it should, they will use approximately the same volume of gas they consumed on the way in (another 70 bar or 1500 litres), and so will arrive at the mouth of the cave within sight of the surface with their pressure gauge showing 70 bar. Their safety cushion of one-third of the

---

[4] As you've doubtless guessed by now, SI units of measurement are used throughout this book, apologies to American readers. But for now, 210 bar is about 3000 psi.

starting volume is intact. They had a good dive, and everything is as it should be: within accepted limits.

It's that simple.

Now what does that mean in terms of distance, which is somewhat easier for most people to understand. Unfortunately, here we run into yet more variables. The most critical is how deep is the cave? Depth has a direct influence on how much gas a diver consumes every minute? Using open circuit SCUBA (regular dive gear and not a rebreather), the deeper one dives, the more gas one consumes with each breath. Not allowing for other stressors, which can affect breathing rates, gas consumption and how long gas will last and so on, for every 10 metres of depth, consumption rate increases in a direct proportion. At 10 metres, it's doubled, at 20 metres it's three times the surface rate, at 30 meters it's four times, and so on.

Let's take for our example right now a dive in one of the highly decorated and shallow caves in Mexico's Quintana Roo Karst country. We can use an average depth of 15 metres which is a realistic average for many of the cave passages there. In the other many other regions, the caves tend to be deeper. In North Florida, for example, an average of about twice that depth would be reasonable.

But for now, in our hypothetical Mexican cave passage, an average diver, on an average day, with an average workload and stress level, using one-third of their starting volume in a couple of 11-liter cylinders, will swim approximately 500 to 600 metres into the cave with this much gas available to use. At the average swimming speed of about 15 metres every minute, that's approximately a 35-minute swim, or 35 minutes from daylight and fresh air. An experienced diver, in the same cave with similar stresses and workload, would go further... perhaps a kilometer or more: a sober thought and a graphic illustration why bolting to the surface in an out-or-air situation is simply not an option in a cave, and why allowing oneself to run low on air is also not an option.

And so, that's how long this particular piece of string is, generally speaking. In short, a cave diver can swim into a cave until she has used one-third (or slightly less) of the volume of gas she started with[5]. Forgive the grammar.

5 I mentioned earlier that I was keeping the explanation of the Rule of Thirds simple for this example, but as with so much involved with limits and cave diving, keeping things simple opens up a sort of mini-sized Pandora's box of complications, which we'll deal with in Question Thirteen. However, for the time-being, we're golden.

Question Seven

*WHAT'S THE MOST IMPORTANT SKILL THAT I
SHOULD LEARN BEFORE I TAKE MY UPCOMING
CAVE CLASS?*

- I guess around 70 percent of students ask this
question either of their chosen cave instructor or the
authorities roaming around the internet forums giving
free advice. There are three answers to this question. In
order they are... (Please read on.)

Breathing is not as simple as it seems. As a group, humans are
shockingly bad at it. Birds are champions – they have a design
advantage – we're just a bunch of also-rans. There are ways for us to
make the best of a bad deal, but that takes effort, which begins with
admitting there's a problem. And that's not intuitively

straightforward. Since we've all been breathing for what passes as adequately for years, so what's the problem?

Apparently, they are legion, and fixing them will make a huge difference, according to the folks teaching us Yoga, Martial Arts, Meditation, Cross-country Skiing, and Tai-Chi.

The folks teaching SCUBA diving, not so much.

The advice in most textbooks is: breathe normally, don't hold your breath. Nothing about how to compensate for breathing through the mouth – not a great start in itself for many of us – plus overcoming the inconvenience of having a regulator stuck in it. (Just in case you are unfamiliar with SCUBA diving gear, a regulator second stage, the thing that goes into a diver's mouth, is bigger and heavier than a hockey puck and attached to the SCUBA tank by a rubber hose, which gets in the way whenever it can. Anything but a <normal> situation!) While breathing on SCUBA does become second nature after a while, that while adds up to several hours at least. One sure sign of a neophyte diver is they haven't learned to trust the regulator and their mouth enough to stop holding the regulator, and perhaps their jaw, in place.

If there is a gap in every major SCUBA agency's curriculum it's here. A freediving course will help, but that's about holding your breath, and because of that, the first priority before the start of any SCUBA class, and certainly a cave class is to learn to breathe.

For the record, I did not learn until I was in my early 20s. A workmate signed me up for a Chinese martial arts program that he'd been recommending to me for months. So, I turned up on a Saturday morning at a mansion tucked away behind century-old sycamore trees in a high-rent North London suburb. I was all bushy-tailed and bright-eyed. This was an exclusive deal. Attendance by invitation only. No walk-in traffic allowed. No visitors. No casual tire-kickers. All very serious, a bit intimidating, and more than a little exciting.

By Sunday afternoon though, I left feeling deflated and completely bummed out. I'd had visions of looking like an extra from a Bruce Lee movie and being able to break oak planks barehanded and snap house bricks in half with two fingers after just one session. That was not to be.

What our small group of newbies got during that first visit was a two-day workshop on Zen philosophy, lectures on the benefits of meditation, and a lot of push-ups, crunches, and squats. Oh, and we had each made a personal seiza bench from precut pieces of poplar banged together with wood glue and hardwood dowels.

I fudged and fumed with disappointment all week. Was it worth going back? Would it get more interesting? Would we learn Kung Fu? How much more carpentry was there going to be?

On the next Thursday afternoon in a pub around the corner from our office, I met with the friend who set the whole thing up for me. We talked. He convinced me to give it another try. Only half convinced, I agreed to 'invest' in one more weekend retreat before giving it up as a bad idea.

The following visit – a couple of weeks later – was not quite the same but similar to the first; still no fighting, but also no woodworking, just two days of breathing. Well, two days of learning basic breathing techniques borrowed from Tai Chi, Qigong, Southern Dragon Kung Fu, Buddhist Anapanasati meditation, and 'sitting'. But this time, rather than feeling disappointed when Sunday evening rolled around, I was starting to 'get it'. I felt good. I even did my homework: more breathing practice; more sitting facing the wall.

Looking back, I forget how many weekends we spent sitting on the benches we made on the first weekend, opening our chest, making sure our ears were aligned with our shoulders, keeping our spines pointing to the sky and breathing, instead of chopping blocks of wood into bits with our hands.

During the several years I ended up attending 'The Mansion', regardless of whether the workshop was about Chinese straight sword technique, Pushing Hands, or Taoist therapeutic movement, every session – morning, afternoon, and nighttime – began with an hour or so 'just' breathing sitting, and trying to 'drop body and mind'.

It became a habit.

I moved away from London more than 40 years ago. I have no idea what happened to the Zen Buddhist retreat tucked away in Barnet, if my Chánshī ever moved back to mainland China or Hong Kong and how he's doing; if my buddy quit working at a London ad agency to study microscopy full-time, or if any of the neophyte martial artists with whom I trained are still 'at it' after so long. I still am... well, the Zazen bit anyway. I have completely given up on the bare-handed wood and house brick splitting business.

Biased because it has worked for me, breathing practice and meditation is a great habit to develop for anyone thinking about taking on the stresses of advanced SCUBA diving. Looking over student materials from several agencies, including the Big Seven, the most detailed advice available seems to be, when on SCUBA breathe normally taking deep slow breaths, and do not skip breathe. (Skip breathing is a foggy-minded attempt by some divers trying to conserve gas by forcing themself to slow their respiration. It usually has the opposite effect achieving little more than increasing carbon-dioxide levels in the blood which leads to a splitting headache.)

There are three simple breathing techniques that will help anyone relax, even the most hyper individuals with 20 browsers windows open in their brain at the same time. And over time, any of these and any combination of them practiced regularly can build other benefits. However, as things to try before diving and as a medium-term preparation for a class, the changes are better than good most folks will find them worthwhile.

These are all simple and effective. The first is a Taoist exercise called Box Breathing. You can do this sitting down (no slouching) or standing. Start with a couple of full breaths in through your nose and out through your mouth through pursed lips (you'll do this nose-mouth switch throughout this exercise), and when you feel ready, breath in deeply for a four-count. (It's unimportant if your four-count is actually four seconds or not; just a four-count that feels comfy and repeatable.) Hold your breath for a four-count. Then exhale for a four-count (clear those lungs). And step four, hold your breath again for a four count. This completes one box. Try to build four boxes at first, and gradually, as you get more comfortable, build up to ten or twenty.

Option two is 4-7-8 breathing. This is another relaxant. Start with a closed mouth and quietly inhale through your nose to a mental count of four. (Again, a count of four, not four seconds; just whatever feels right for you). Hold your breath for a count of seven. Exhale through pursed lips again (you can make a sound if you wish) for a count of eight. Repeat the process six more times for a total of seven breath cycles.

The final one is my favourite and if you have done any form of structured meditation (any form of Buddhist meditation, Dhyāna, other Yoga practices, or freediving), this should be familiar. This is counting breath meditation 101. Start by sitting comfortably. You don't have to adopt a full lotus position or anything as formal for this to work, but a straight back and head positioned squarely on your shoulders will help. Many teachers suggest closing one's eyes when doing this. I was taught to have my eyes slightly open and looking at (but not seeing) a spot about two meters in front of me. How you approach this is up to you. There are no meditation police in sight.

Now take a few deep breaths, settle your body until you're comfortable, shuffle from side-to-side if that helps, and try to quieten your thoughts. Begin to breath normally, just a relaxed rhythm, certainly a nice slow tempo but not forced and definitely not purposeful. Focus your attention on the air flowing in and out of your nose. (Mouth closed for this exercise.)

When you feel ready and your breath is coming and going easily, start to count. One on the inhale, two on the exhale. Three on the inhale, four on the exhale. And so on until ten. When you count ten and exhale, go back to one. Keep this up for five minutes. And if your mind drifts and you lose the count, no worries, bring your attention back to breathing and start counting from one again.

It's that simple. Deceptively so. If someone says they don't have time to spend five minutes on this exercise a day, the correct answer I'm told is: "Well, then, you need to do it for ten minutes!"

I remain unable to break wooden planks with my palms nor can I execute a "one-inch punch" to chop house bricks in two, but the habit of sitting quietly every day for 20 minutes or so, has been instructive and helpful. I recommend it!

An important note: since one has to be mindful of the first rule of diving – don't hold your breath – these are intended to be practiced out of the water. There are a couple of suggestions for 'in-water exercises' towards the last few notes of the Fourth Movement: Control your breath and you control panic.

SITUATIONAL AWARENESS (SA)

For anybody who takes part in a high-risk activity that's equipment-intensive, and that happens someplace well removed from a sedate park bench in full spring sunshine, feeding ducks, a real asset is having a well-developed sixth sense, a Spidey Sense to tell when something's about to go pear-shaped before it actually goes pear-shaped. The formal term for this skill is situational awareness or SA. For someone who's decided to play around for fun inside a cave, it's a vital skill.

Situational awareness (SA) is something we know all about, even if we're unfamiliar with the term, because it is innate: built into and part of our makeup. It's one of the kaleidoscope of things that makes us people. When some early hominid grandmother climbed down from the relative safety of her tree-nest and decided to run around in the grass to hunt for lunch or an afternoon snack, situational awareness kept her alive. The unaware, didn't make it back up to hang around and chat with their neighbours in the jungle canopy that evening.

They ended up as something else's lunch or afternoon snack.

SA is understanding the environment, and its potential to harm or surprise. In a team dynamic, SA also covers the elements of the team – its members – and how they'll react to changes and challenges. SA is critical since it effects decisions made by oneself and one's teammates at that precise moment and projected into the near future.

Doctor Mica Endsley describes SA as: "...the perception of the elements in the environment within a volume of time and space, the comprehension of their meaning, and the projection of their status in the near future". Her work describing, refining, and teaching SA as chief scientist for the US Air Force was definitive: she is the subject matter expert *sans-pareil*. And it is the" projection of future status" that's a potential lifesaver for a diver in a cave. In short form, hearing the familiar sound of a fan spinning and a shovel scrapping.

There are fewer better signs than the look in your partner's eyes, and failing that for a diver on open circuit, a good tell is to take note of any change in your partner's respiration rate. Watch the bubbles. Apparently, the average human at rest breaths between 12 and 15 times a minute. For a relaxed diver, that's probably high; last time in a cave, mine was around six and my buddy's was five. But in any case, knowing what's normal for a buddy and seeing it change, should send up a flag of some colour other than green.

Given western society's current fixation with mindfulness, perhaps SA may be easier to explain using an old Zen story. When visiting his Roshi, a monk was greeted formally, and when the conversation turned to the monk's progress in building awareness, the old master asked: "When you entered, you left your walking stick by the door, did you not?" The monk answered that he had. The

Roshi continued: "On which side of the door did you leave it?" And of course, the monk couldn't recall and therefore lacked true awareness.

One of my cave-diving Roshis, a guy called Larry Green, taught me the missing gear awareness lesson during my cave instructor apprenticeship with him. During the few minutes of total calmness at the end of a dive class, when the whole class would be hanging in the cavern area, he would swim around 'stealing' backup lights, reels, anything he could from their respective harnesses. Then he would get their attention and slowly hand back mission-critical equipment, one piece at a time.

Sometimes described as the chess player's mentality, SA, another perspective is to think that as a diver one is always drawn to play the black pieces and Murphy, or his evil proxy, is playing white and has the first move. In cave diving, the environment, and sometimes the instructor, is an evil proxy waiting to trip wake up the ill-prepared with a whack from a keisaku in one form or another. Therefore, gaining leverage to overcome the white-first-move advantage is a recommended practice before sitting down at the chess board or planning a dive. SA is the answer.

A final thought on the subject of SA. The internet's favourite guru, Jagadish Vasudev, a sort of modern-day Maharishi Mahesh Yogi, and better known as Sadhguru, said: "A situation is neither positive nor negative... Every situation demands a different kind of response [that is all]. Just be aware." That sums things up neatly.

QUIET HANDS AND FEET

Several years ago, I wrote a book called The Six Skills specifically to give to students who'd signed up for technical diving classes with me. It was intended as a primer to help them prepare for what I thought of as my gentle and avuncular way of teaching, but that possibly was anything but. In any case, one of the skills it highlighted was the ability to float in the water column without effort or thought.

One might be tempted to say, "like a fish", which is a nice thought, but of course fish do not need a drysuit; thermal undies; a sidemount harness; a bum-bag filled with backup lights and sundry bits and pieces; a pigtail filled with line markers; a few spools of cave line; a backup mask; two aluminum cylinders fitted with regulators and spgs; primary lights, and the other paraphernalia necessary for us to visit their home. So, perhaps different to a fish, but with similar ease.

And that is my suggestion for the third skill to have some proficiency with, before venturing into a cave diver course. But like so many skills, it requires fluency in several others: having excellent buoyancy control; having equipment under control and in trim; being comfortable in the water; breathing properly; moving – when the time comes to move – precisely, with the least possible fuss.

There are exercises to help arrive at this spot, but none can be rushed. They require practice, patience, and the passage of time. Wasn't it Lancelot 'Capability' Brown, the 18th century English landscape artist who said, "The perfect lawn takes a handful of grass seed, a heavy roller, and 300 years"? Certainly not that much time, perhaps, but patience, nevertheless.

A good starting point is being familiar with one's gear to the point of being able to operate every function faultlessly, flawlessly, and with no hesitation, which is one reason that cave divers fuss so much over the exact position of clips, valves, buttons, straps, knobs, and hoses. As mentioned, practice and patience...time in the water.

I guess a summary answer to the original question asking what skills to have prior to starting a cave diving class should start by suggesting humility. Having the grace and appreciation to understand the limitations of being a human in the water; or more simply, to be a conscious, mindful, and respectful diver.

Yes, since we're looking at what skills a student cave diver needs, that'll work.

Question Eight

WHAT'S THE MAIN ATTRACTION FOR WHAT YOU
DO: IS THERE MORE TO CAVE DIVING THAN WET
ROCKS? DID YOU EVER SEE ANIMALS OR CAVE ART
WHILE DIVING?

- Following the miracle cave rescue of the boys and
their soccer coach in Thailand – especially after the
release of the movies – the profile of cave diving has
grown as has interest in whatever it is that attracts
people to do it. That story painted a bleak picture of
the pastime. And as for prehistoric cave painting, I can't
remember who it was that first asked about cave art,
but the question comes up fairly regularly.

Our sense of smell is the most evocative. Sight, touch, hearing, and
taste are concrete, corporeal. Smells, however, confuse the front of
our brain and take a shortcut through an accident of anatomy,
arriving instantly and directly at the gates of our limbic system and

brain regions that manage emotion and memory. It's as though the olfactory bulb blossoms every time we smell something different. It opens like an innocent and sends out information without any restrictions or filters. It broadcasts with unchained vigor. And that starts a sensory wave of memory, visceral and emotional, dug up sometimes from a deep past: a so-called Proustian moment. *"À la recherche du temps perdu"*.

We all have special smells that trigger what Proust called lost times. Lavender, the sweet and subtle little blue flowers, always sends me back to Epsom, in Surrey, and great-aunt Alice's front room in a rambling late-Victorian house filled with tortoiseshell picture frames, occasional tables draped in lace, jardiniere with huge potted palms and aspidistra guarding its hallway.

That's my recall to a lost time: my involuntary memory.

There are others, dozens, or hundreds of them. The smell of apricot jam recalls a schoolboy trip to northern Spain. The damp earthy smell after rain, the only one with its special name: petrichor, the blood of the immortals. That smell takes me to Lords cricket ground in North London: the home of a different breed of immortals. The smell of city dust and honeysuckle: that's St. James Cathedral in downtown Toronto in late July. Each of these oddly intense and persistent.

The strangest though – and a direct link to what's attractive about caves and indirectly to the presence of cave art – is the scent of floor polish (a specific one I cannot name but recognize), brewed coffee, and the crispy smell of French tobacco. All that reminds me of a single visit to Lascaux II in the Dordogne. The involuntary memory that it conjures is a mixture of fascination, distress, and sorrow. Lascaux II is a very fancy museum housing reproductions of the cave art found in *Grotte de Lascaux*. The Lascaux cave itself is the site of what's perhaps the most famous collection of Upper Palaeolithic cave art ever discovered. There are hundreds of animal paintings and even more engravings.

The cave entrance is just a few steps from the museum, but it is closed these days. Locked up tight and dark. The exhaled breath, perfume, sweat, the simple presence of visitors changed the micro-climate when it was open to the general public, threatening to extinguish its tenuous link to a collective, creative past. I did not visit it then. I missed my chance. And access now is limited to one person annually. This single visitor is allowed in to monitor the slow cancerous mold destroying the real art lining the cave's walls and ceiling. Not even scientists get to visit, so entry for a wannabe tool-shed archaeologist like me now, is certainly not possible.

However, getting into the museum is easy, and every week thousands pay a few Euros to do it. It's worth the price. The quality of the images is amazing. We're told the artists who did the reproduction work used similar materials to the early humans who created the originals 17,000 years ago. Iron oxide (dried blood perhaps), ochre, charcoal, urine, spit.

Somebody somewhere tried really, really hard to fill the museum displays as closely as possible with the magnificence of the real things; and they are stunning. Huge and expansive. As expressive in pure form and simple line as a Matisse drawing; better, earlier, original. But of course, what's missing is the authentic smell of a cave: unique and unforgettable. The meticulous attention to detail in the visual copies has fallen down on the Proustian register.

The visceral link to another past is not there, and visitors have to be content with the faint whiff of Gitanes, coffee and cleaning products.

But, I'm searching for the essence of caves' appeal: especially the ones that one can dive.

I've loved caves since before I can remember. My parents on a holiday tour of England's Mendip Hills and Cheddar Gorge, lost me to a cave. I was five or six and have no memory of my detour into the underground. Decades later, over a shared meat pie and a beer, my father told me I disappeared for several minutes into what he said was a small crack in the limestone. They found me because I was "barking like a bloody dog". I have no idea why, and nor did he, but it had no lasting ill-effect and no puppies were harmed in the process. As a slightly older kid, able to walk into a cave without alarming anyone, and without feeling the urge to do wolf impersonations once inside, I played at dry caving in England's west country and across the Welsh border in Dan yr Ogof. Caves totally fascinated me. I didn't give much thought back then to what went into the appeal of damp and dark holes in the ground for me. But the smell was, and is, a part of it.

Genevieve von Petzinger, a Canadian paleoanthropologist and self-described 'rock art researcher', who strives to interpret Ice Age cave paintings, says: "There's just something about caves that feels otherworldly", and explains that deep inside any cave it's hard not to let your imagination run wild. Petzinger describes the barrier between the seen and the unseen world; the world of the shaman and the link between the supernatural and the rest of us, what she calls "the membrane that separates the supernatural and the mundane", is thin in there. Petzinger is one of the folks who gets it. She digs the secret darkness, its smells, and its colours.

Yes, colours, but not the colours of paint; the colours in the rock itself.

When a cave's history includes the happy accident of having a dry period – and that period is measured in thousands of human lifetimes – things grow. Collectively we call those things <cave furniture> or speleothems. They're the stone formations left behind by mineral-rich rainwater as it drips down walls, off ceilings, and bounces on the floor. It leaves behind calcite, halite, and gypsum which form flowstones, stalactites, helictites, curtains, stalagmites, columns, soda straws and other deposits, each with a special name to describe it.

The morphology is complex, something close to 3000 distinct forms, but as Richard Feynman told us, knowing the name of something doesn't mean you understand it, or that you appreciate its beauty, or comprehend what it can tell us about history and past climate.

And so it is with cave decorations. They are beautiful, forming the most complex shapes, and the palate that geology paints them with varies from pure white, like royal icing on a Christmas cake, to the colour of straw, the red of Rudolph's nose, the blue of cornflowers, and buttercup yellow.

But, to the question: what's the big attraction? I don't know where else to start except Quintana Roo, Mexico.

Let's go to one of the little restaurants on the main drag in Tulum. Not the beach road, but into one of the little places beside Highway 307 as it runs arrow-straight through the center of town. Let's sit there under a palapa, huge TVs showing the most outrageously camp music videos, and wait. Sooner or later, they will come in and we can ask. Yes, cave divers will walk in, order tacos and a Modelo Especial or Bohemia, and the cazón empanadas, and we can ask: "What's so attractive about the caves; and how come you dive in them? The ocean is just a few kilometers over there." And we can point east. "Why not dive there with the whale sharks and turtles?"

Everyone will have their own reasons: the challenge, the majesty, the uniqueness, to be close to Mother Earth, to be enveloped in history, to visit an alien world. But secretly at the heart of it is an odd sensation that we belong in there. One of them will say something about being inside a cave feels like home: safe and comforting; consistent and dependable; stable and spectacularly enduring; a place of belonging. They might compare it to a temple, a church, a holy place.

Wouldn't that be a strange thing?

THE WATER HAS WASHED IT AWAY, BUT THERE ARE FIREPITS AND MINES AND THE BONES OF LOST ANIMALS

Unfortunately, we do not see any sign of the classic cave art in Mexico's flooded caves. (Nor is there any I know of in the caves in the Bahamas which have a similar geological history, and which are as spectacular.) So, there is nothing like the amazing drawings found in dry caves in Spain and France. No Stone Age Sistine Chapels, no frescos, and certainly nothing to rival what's found in Europe or Africa.

Paleoindians may have decorated these caves when they were dry; when glaciers covered North America to the 45th parallel, and sea level was 30 meters lower than where it sits today. Perhaps there was a *Grotte de Lascaux* in the Yucatan or the Bahamas back then. But we'll never know because the rising water levels and the subsequent action of water over thousands of years would have washed away any trace, if it ever existed. There is research ongoing in the hope of finding bas-relief carvings of animals, similar to ones worked into limestone walls and ceilings in European caves. Perhaps one day soon, something will turn up.

However, there is Mexican cave art. It depicts different images. Not herds of horses, aurochs and antelopes populating tales of hunter-gatherers, but a different vocabulary; written in the same ochre and charcoal, blood, and urine, but these are the product of a different epoch and another mindset. The paintings were found by a team of archaeologists, led by Sergio Grosjean Abimerhi. He is an anthropologist and environmentalist whose activism has resulted in massive clean-ups and the removal of tonnes of junk from cenotes in the region. The cave paintings found by Grosjean and his colleagues, which he calls, "the most significant of its kind in the state", are a collection of symbols and signs in a rock shelter in the region. Geometrical, graphic, something not quite like hieroglyphs but related. These date from less than 1000 years ago and so they are Mayan: not prehistoric, simply pre-Columbian.

They're like their earlier European counterparts – what Genevieve von Petzinger studies – and like those, their meaning is totally obscure. For now.

So, while cave divers don't get to enjoy cave art, there is evidence of early human activity in the caves.

Local explorers, Fred Devos and Sam Mecham recently discovered evidence of mining in a handful of popular caves in the Yucatan. During the Pleistocene-Holocene transition (which is the period when the earth's climate started to warm up signalling the end of the Ice Age) early humans were digging in the caves to extract ochre. Ochre is a mixture of iron oxide, clay, and sand; a base pigment to make the paint our ancestors used to decorate sacred objects, themselves, pottery, jewelry, and the walls of caves.

Scientists believe it was mined during a 2,000-year period using speleothems (stalactites and stalagmites broken from the cave floor and ceiling) as digging tools, since the whole of that area has few if any outcrops of hard rocks such as flint and chert that Stone Age people in other areas used to make hand axes, knives, and other tools. Regardless, miners excavated masses of rocks from the floor of the caves, and estimates are they quarried thousands of tonnes of ochre during that period.

Also, in several caves there are the charred remains of fires built around the same period, and piles of broken cave furniture that experts think was used as navigation.

So, is there cave art in the caves divers visit? Not really. And what's the attraction of a flooded cave besides wet rocks? That depends on how you look at it.

A NOTE ON THE CREATURES LIVING IN CAVES

Caves, both dry and wet, are full of life. Much of it tiny, fragile, and to our eyes, odd and insignificant. Odd because cave dwelling animals lack pigment and under the bright illumination of a cave diver's light are transparent, blind, and surprised. Insignificant because of our ignorance.

This subterranean fauna, stygofauna, live in water-filled spaces deep underground and are creatures of the real dark, some of which may have lived there for longer than we or any of our hominid ancestors have walked the planet's surface.

These are mostly invertebrates: shrimp, isopods crayfish, amphipods, and crustaceans the size of a human baby's little fingernail. There are fish too. Some lost after swimming in from outside, but some true cave dwellers, without pigment or eyes.

They are unique. In cave systems in just one area of the Bahamas, there are more than 500 species of stygobitic isopods particular to that region. While diving caves in a remote region of Brazil, our little team of duffers discovered several species of fish new to science.

So, I'm not sure we have any idea how many genera and undescribed species of water-dwelling creatures there are in caves around the world, but we do know there's a lot of scope for serious research in the darkness.

A PERSONAL PERSPECTIVE

There is another addition to any list of things that cave diving delivers besides views of yet-to-be-discovered animals and highly attractive wet rocks. But this is a totally personal view and a little off the wall – although I know several cave divers who feel more or less the same way.

I make no excuse for being a big fan and flag-waving campaigner for meditation. I put an hour or so aside every morning to 'sit and practice'. It clears my mind, adds focus to the day, helps me deal with the personal demons and PTSD I have following me around – you may have the same sort of entourage.

But all that time on the cushion is practice. That's what it's called and that's what it is. A less enlightened buddy once asked what the practice is for and added something about levitation and nirvana. And of course, that's not it at all. It's practice for everything that's around us now... all this, what we see every day, the so-called real world.

In his excellent book on Vipassana[6] meditation, *Mindfulness in Plain English*, Bhante Gunaratana writes that the goal of all that sitting and non-thinking is to carry what's practiced and learned while meditating and sitting on a cushion, into everyday life. "Driving on the Freeway, doing the dishes...". Mindfulness at one level is about building awareness: situational awareness, a handy skill in a cave.

And from my perspective, one of the huge benefits of all the personal time invested studying and becoming familiar with mindfulness, is taking it with me into the secret places that caves lead to.

While this may be difficult for some to process – and perhaps it was slightly different when I was teaching and there were other factors at play – but certainly now, the internal effects of being underground and the bits of my conscious mind it opens up, is why I dive caves.

---

[6] While I have every respect for Vipassana meditation, I follow a different path.

And as I read this back to myself, I realise there is something important about the attraction of caves that is missing from this rather odd, lopsided list. There are several special caves where one can swim over the remains of some long-extinct animal. Not some dead sea creature embedded in the walls or ceiling of the cave as a fossilised exclamation. Not the tell-tale remains of a sea fan, or a crinoid, or a perfectly symmetrical echinoid from the late Ordovician. But the bones of animals that some early human ancestor would have known. The giant bones of megafauna like cave bears, glyptodons, giant sloths, and daedons. Creatures that wandered around when the caves were dry, and ice covered much of the world. And always one wonders how these animals, jungle dwellers, wandered hundreds of metres from daylight to the back of a cave to die. What drove them to enter the cave? Was it Paleoindian hunters? Another predictor? Curiosity? And how long did they search for the lost exit in the dark?

The first time I dived on the wreck of the Empress of Ireland, a British ocean liner sunk near the mouth of the St. Lawrence River in Quebec, Canada, my buddy and I imagined we could hear the voices of the thousand or so passengers that went down with her. Were those whispers the effects of inert gas narcosis, or simply an over-stimulated imagination? Memorable either way.

The sounds of less human grief but a voice nevertheless, there's something to be said for hovering over the remains of an extinct being with bones the size of a character from a Flintstones cartoon. Those too have something interesting to tell us.

Count one more reason to dive caves.

Question Nine

ARE ALL EXPLORERS LONERS? WHAT MAKES THEM DO IT? DO CAVE DIVERS DIVE ALONE? ISN'T THAT AGAINST THE RULES?

- It was at a book signing that was part of a dive show somewhere in Middle America – one of the rectangular states – and a couple with book in hand meandered up and asked for it to be signed and dedicated; they were both recreational divers and avid fish-nerds with cameras. The woman said: "We were pleasantly surprised by your presentation... we thought all explorers were terrible loners; whereas you work with people and seem to like them!"

I'm an only child; no brothers, no sisters. My only siblings growing up were various household pets: dogs, cats, budgies, and so on. My parents were animal lovers: kids, well... just the one was enough for them. So, yes, an only child: a lucky one, by some accounts. I heard a guest on public radio recently talking about the "deep trauma" carried by kids raised as singles, without human-type brothers and sisters. That's surprising news. I had none of that. Instead, I thought it was a special treat being the only kid in the house. No sibling rivalry to buzzkill the vibe. Nobody using my 'stuff' without asking, and no little brothers or sisters getting greasy fingerprints on my toys.

Most of all, and something carried into adulthood on a flaming chariot with trumpets and fireworks, the freedom to do what one pleases without needing to ask permission or hand out invitations. Certainly, there was trauma. But it came from growing up in a classist society, during the Cold War, mid-way between the Atomic Weapons Research Establishment at Aldermaston and RAF Greenham Common, where a resident fleet of US nuclear bombers sat ready to take flight and unleash Armageddon.

In essence, there were concerns living at what passed for Ground Zero to anyone with a big red button on their desk. So, trauma enough, but none of it connected with being *un enfant unique*, and nothing associated with being asked to carry the awkward stereotypical baggage that characterizes only children as selfish loners with poor social skills. That nonsense didn't even show up on community radar.

My partner is also an only child with similar non-conforming behaviour and social outlook. She's a therapist and that brings a special sort of trauma, but it too is thanks to something other than growing up without siblings.

Unfortunately, she hates olives and anchovies, so Pasta Puttanesca and Caesar salads are difficult; however, apart from that, we're very similar. And so, based on our respective characters and life choices, neither of us fit the old-school stereotypes associated with only children.

Combine that with the stack of present-day research telling us that being an only child does not significantly affect personality traits as much as was once thought, and there's some adjustment to be made.

The fact is, there is no significant difference in personality between only children and children with siblings. So, all those old myths and assumptions about loner behaviour should be blown out of the water.

I'd say the same is true of the myths about explorers and adventurers; those cheeky buccaneers who do crazy things like sticking their heads above society's parapets.

For anyone who thinks these folks are anti-social losers, cavalier about risk, who harbour a death wish, and have poor self-control – perhaps akin to my camera-toting book-loving fans from the Mid-West – the reality comes as a surprise. Anything deeper than a cursory glance points to a very different breed of person.

The seat of the issue is society's slack, pejorative definition of 'loner' and what it means. Einstein said that being a loner "...gives you time to wonder, to search for the truth. Have holy curiosity".

We should reposition the way we think about those of us who are perfectly comfortable doing what we do alone. If that makes someone a loner, then the social dictionary needs a modest more inclusive rewrite.

THE EXPLORER GENE

But the misunderstanding is forgivable. Someone pasted the social-media equivalent of a 'serial risk taker' label on the cave diving community's collective back. A sort of 'kick me' prank, and just as juvenile and unfair. Most of the community, if not exactly fitting the definition of totally risk-averse, at very least follow a cautious approach. It's made clear to them in the literature, their training, and as a community, that the environment quickly punishes anyone with a sloppy attitude towards risk management.

Of course, there are exceptions. Some folks colour outside the guidelines either because of bloody-minded ignorance, or a misguided sense of immunity, but taken as a whole the technical diving, and especially the cave diving community, frowns at the foolhardy.

It could do better. Gareth Lock, the man behind the very clever Human Diver initiative, certainly thinks so. He works at fostering, what he terms "an inclusive culture", and putting distance between SCUBA divers of all stripes and "unintended outcomes".

His influence is growing, yet the dare-devil labelling endures.

What's unfair is that we all have a touch of the explorer in us; part of our character that kicks against the traces? Well, perhaps not all of us. Not everyone. We all have that friend who isn't open to trying new foods, travelling to new places, or chasing new discoveries. They stay home wrapped in a blanket reading about adventure rather than experiencing it. But for the rest of us, there is plenty of curiosity to keep us a little restless, and buzzy.

Geneticists have isolated a gene they've tagged DRD4. It regulates dopamine levels in the brain and that's linked to how we feel pleasure, satisfaction, motivation, and how we sense reward. When we do something that gives us pleasure – eating ice-cream, taking the dog for a walk on a sunny day – dopamine is what floods our brain to tell us, "That was fun! Let's do that again!"

A variant of that gene – known as DRD4-7R and called the explorer gene by some – is expressed by around 20 percent of us. It's thought that those folks, the ones with this variant, do not get the "regular" dose of dopamine as a reward for doing "regular" activities that the other eighty percent find completely gratifying. And this slight deficiency tends to make them more restless, more curious, and intrepid by nature. Research shows that those with this gene variant, embrace movement, change, and adventure. These are the crowd seeking the rush of discovery and the thrill of travel. Their 'normal' is a little more extreme: nailing a set of moguls on a ski hill, hiking in Nepal, laying line in a new section of cave. These folks have increased curiosity and restlessness and are more likely to take on a personal quest for adventure and excitement in their lives.

If you have ever been told you are dopamine deficient – which sounds like an insult in some odd way – this is what was meant. So not an insult at all. You get your kicks from stuff that does not fit comfortably inside the 'regular' box.

Perhaps being a cave diver is mostly about this 7R variant. Studies in animals simulating 7R's actions, have shown an increase for movement and novelty, so, perhaps it's so. Perhaps it's all about DRD4-7R and being adventurous or not is totally due to a single genetic deviation, the same as owning an observable human characteristic like curly hair or an attached earlobe.

But surely there's more to it than that. There have to be other considerations. The drive to indulge a natural capacity for adventure and wanderlust has to be combined with the physical ability to act on those impulses. One also has to enjoy life; circumstances and the freedom from mainstream society's expectations and responsibilities – as well as the mindset – to make it happen.

It may be pure coincidence and a fluke that so many cave explorers who base themselves in Cave Country – regardless of which cave country in question – are 'from away'. They are ex-pats, immigrants, folks who carry a passport that's a different flavour to the one they had at birth. It's said that this too is the sort of thing that people with 7R are more likely to do with their lives. They are more likely to pull up roots and wander. Perhaps there's a potential PhD thesis for someone in that rabbit hole.

DO CAVE DIVERS WORK ALONE?

But the question was, do cave divers work alone. Is it a solitary pastime? The short answer is: Not as a general rule, but it depends.

Even before taking their first breath on SCUBA , the message every would-be diver gets from textbooks, Google searches or their instructor is that one must always dive with a friend, a buddy: always, always. This is true of every diver certification agency – all 120 of them – but especially from all of the Big Seven: the ones who own eighty to ninety percent of the market. It's a sort of covenant. Diving is a team thing, an experience that MUST be shared with a friend.

Diving with a friend is called "following the buddy system", and all basic recreational SCUBA training and diving lore is tightly wound around it. To stray from this system, to dive alone, is an anathema; and to question its doctrine is the highest form of heresy.

And then a guy called Bret Gilliam, threw all that out of the window.

Gilliam, was a visionary, and gold-standard individualist with a solid background in the business of diving and a hatred of complacency as deep as his one-time world-record deep dive, was the owner of Scuba Diving International (SDI), a respected training agency and one of the largest; a member of the Big Seven. Sometime around 1999, he directed his staff to develop a program that went against everything dive agencies had been pushing to their students since the beginning of time: the buddy system. It was called "Solo Diver" and was billed as a complete program dealing with the equipment, mind-set, skills, and protocols necessary to dive successfully (and safely) without a buddy.

His rationale was that "divers dive solo all the time". Sometimes, he reasoned, they know they're on their own, and more often, they have no idea they're on their own because relying on the person in the water beside them to offer useful assistance in an emergency, was as dependable as a chocolate teacup. "The buddy system is a wonderful idea, but it doesn't suit everyone or every circumstance".

By questioning the status quo, Gilliam shared that nasty secret, that the industry as a whole at that stage, was very cagey about sharing. By doing so, Gilliam and SDI were at the pointy end of a latter-day Exsurge Domini: the SCUBA diving equivalent to a papal bull that charged him and his agency with deviation from the teachings and practices of the church of recreational SCUBA diving.

Unlike Martin Luther, the recipient of the original wrist slap from Pope Leo X, Gilliam wasn't given 60 days to recant before full excommunication; it was instantaneous. But just like Luther, he didn't care. He was done with what he'd labelled the "hypocrisy and myopia", propping up the traditional buddy system.

"I can't say that everyone dives solo, but it's a common thing to do; but agencies, instructors, industry people generally, just deny it happens." Gilliam called this broken logic and silliness.

THE EVOLUTION OF A BETTER BUDDY SYSTEM

When the dust settled, many of us saw Gilliam's solo diver program, in spite of its label, as a pretty thorough course in how to be a better dive buddy; an updated and overdue approach to creating stronger ties between divers, and the start of building a better general understanding what makes a strong dive team. And Gilliam, a savvy marketing guy (or maybe it was pure coincidence), timed the launch of his solo diver program to coincide with the growth of technical diving and its 'out of the closet emergence' into the industry's mainstream.

And today, there are many similar courses to SDI's Solo Diver offered by most of the larger dive agencies. The only constant is change; and perhaps a business model of follow-the-leader. But they use a label less contentious than Solo Diver.

However, for technical divers, and perhaps especially cave divers, there are occasions when diving as an *enfant unique* is necessary. However, more often, reliance on a form of the buddy system is *de rigour*, albeit a version of that system modified to suit their special needs. As you might guess, it's a seriously beefed-up version.

REDUNDENCY

Extra gas, an extra mask, back-up lights and computer, spare bits and pieces in a pocket or pouch, and a second buddy, is what makes a technical diver, and especially a cave diver, happy.

So, to satisfy that habit, the perfect team for cave diving is not the traditional two-person team that Gilliam questioned and offered an alternative to, and not that one solo-diver alternative, but three!

Three like-minded and similarly focused divers is touted as the safest option. This gives a third opinion creating the dive plan, another hand prepping for the dive, extra help during an emergency, another person to share the overall experience with. Essentially, the benefit of a three-person team is: Everyone has a buddy and a back-up buddy. Redundancy personified. Something worth thinking about at all levels of diving, perhaps?

Choosing who's on the team though is key. Another of those old technical diving tropes was, 'don't dive with idiots'; a simplification to the cave manual's suggestion to 'choose mature, balanced, careful and conservative buddies as dive partners'.

Certainly, the norm is to pick dive buddies who have the appropriate training, a familiarity with the kit and protocols required on the dive, and recent experience in similar conditions (not some similar-ish dives from three years ago). Also, making sure one's buddies – whose understanding of the roles and responsibilities of teamwork – mesh with everyone else's.

Oddly, I was taught that when diving as one of a three-person team, the weakest diver leads. At first this seems silly, faulty advice, but the logic behind it is sound. It works, especially in a cave because if one of the goals of the dive is to gain experience and enjoy that process, the person leading sets the pace, takes responsibility for navigation (leaving a breadcrumb trail and so on), and decides when to turn the dive and head home (normal gas management rules considered). All this while having the reassurance there are two stronger divers backing them up and 'overseeing' their decisions.

The secret sauce that makes 'the weakest leads' system work is defining what weakest and strongest mean. Obvious differentiators are which buddy has the highest number of dives, the most time in the water. Another consideration is who best knows the dive site (the cave system). But there are other factors too; loads of them.

Among a true peer group strength could come down to whose primary light has the weakest charge or throws the least light, who has the least gas, who has a dodgy knee, who has heated drysuit undies and who is diving in a wetsuit, who had tacos for breakfast...take your pick. But perhaps the most frequent decider when a buddy team are equally experienced, is who's up to carry the reels, spools, extra line markers, and is happy to manage them today?

There is certainly a zeitgeist to working as a team, and while individual talent is fine, more can be accomplished, and more challenges conquered successfully as a member of a functional team, rather than a bunch of individuals all taking a crack at it.

So, yes, explorers (and let's agree that to some extent all experienced cave divers meet that definition) can function alone, but often choose not to, and this makes this group really difficult to pigeonhole. And that seems to make sociologists uncomfortable.

Albert Einstein suggested that being a loner opens wonder to our search for meaning. It's a precursor to being curious and will "make your life worth living". However, there is a world of difference between understanding theoretical physics and cave diving.

Question Ten

I CERTIFIED RECENTLY WITH **** AND MY OPEN WATER INSTRUCTOR WAS A GENIUS. A SUPERWOMAN. WHY CAN'T SHE TEACH ME TO CAVE DIVE? SHE TOLD ME I AM A NATURAL DIVER, SO I THINK I'M READY. IS THERE SOME FORM OR SOMETHING SHE NEEDS TO FILL OUT SO THAT WE CAN GO CAVE DIVING?

- Scuba diving is fun. Teaching people to do it can be a unique thrill, a rare treat, and it often is. It's also not that alone. Done with conviction and a professional attitude there's the constant opportunity for personal growth, and that opportunity is open to every SCUBA instructor at every level. And perhaps this side benefit – personal growth – is the most important thing for a would-be instructor, and that instructor's students, to consider. However, teaching people to dive deserves to be more than a side hustle, especially at an advanced level like cave diving. Not every instructor has

the ability (or professional qualifications) to teach diving
in a cave, and that thought leads to the summary
question: 'What actually makes for a good instructor,
and what should I look for in one?' I think that's a great
place to start. Let's find the right instructor for a
pretend diver we'll call Sam.

Have you ever wondered about the difference between a prodigy, a
genius, and someone who gets called 'a natural' because they
perform some skill or another beautifully well. That skill could be
surfing the big waves off the coast of Portugal, juggling chainsaws, or
our those 'mastered' by a newly certified open water diver?

Between the first two, my guess is that it's simply a question
of age. It seems birthdays are all that's at the bottom of it. To
deserve the prodigy listing in one's personal bio, one needs to be a
Mozart reincarnation who can sit on a piano stool and smash out the
equivalent of Minuet and Trio in G major, at age six. Or an
alternative is to be that TikTok eight-year-old who picks up a
Telecaster and riffs a Jimmy Page solo, note for note, without
breaking a sweat.

On the other hand, we apply the genius label for a grown-up
talent. Since we seem to be talking about copying greatness as
homage (producing a pastiche so to speak), perhaps we can define
genius as someone with the ability to knock-off a dozen stanzas of
metaphysical poetry *a la* John Dunne for an English Lit. thesis; or an
art school graduate who can paint a convincing David Hockney look-
alike and wind-up with a finished canvas perfect in every detail
except its provenance.

Maybe a prodigy's neurons are wired differently to everyone else's. Maybe a genius has no filtering system between their unconscious and conscious mind. Perhaps they both express a variant protein or a freaky enzyme that allows them to process more information per second than the rest of us. The big difference being that prodigies have the gift from birth, but geniuses have to wait until puberty, or passing some other major life waypoint for their special gift to kick in.

Ellen Winner, Professor Emerita of Psychology at Boston College, tells us what drives success more than other factors is the "rage to master". She says it's an insatiable desire to get better at something specific.

This, because talent alone is not enough. We are all talented at one thing or another, but few of us can call ourselves prodigies or geniuses. That leaves the majority of us as also-rans. But all is not lost because if we too have the rage to master, we may earn a status extraordinary enough to lead the pack when performing something epic, and look surprisingly and totally natural when doing it.

Talent alone does not manifest itself as a Mozart-like sonata, a Pink Floyd rock classic, a painting with colour as pure as Hockney's by default, or to be competent enough to look natural while showing off our talent. Talent has to be pursued and worked at, or it just rattles around inside one's head, knocking flower vases off tables and taking up space.

Professor Winner, whose research explores the psychology of art, tells us that a strong work ethic is a start but leveraging talent and producing "a domain-specific, exceptional result", takes something more. She tells us that being extraordinary only happens to folks who are "hard driving, focused, dominant, independent risk takers, with a willingness to toil and tolerate frustration and persist in the face of failure".

So, it seems, according to science, the common denominator on the pathway from ordinary to greatness is pig-headedness, hard work, dedicated practice, and an unwavering focus. Excellence of any and every flavour boils down to time spend sitting at the piano keyboard. It's time playing scales again and again and again until one's fingers bleed; it's having a trashcan, either real or digital, filled with rejected attempts at getting it right; it's about rejection and having the resolve to carry on without self-pity or blame. Emile Zola, it's said, had a sign in the study of his chateau outside Paris that read, *Nulla dies sine linea*[7]*:* which loosely translates for a writer into, no days without putting something on paper. And it was Zola who said: "The artist is nothing without the gift, but the gift is nothing without work".

Which leaves us space once again to think that really, it's all about investing time and using it to practice...lots.

That's why when someone tells me their open water instructor was a genius, my scepticism meter swings into the red zone. I also have issues with calling someone a natural diver. It isn't because someone teaching students the very basic, starting-from-the-ground-up course, couldn't possibly be a genius. There's a chance they might be. And it's not because calling someone a natural when they are taking their first steps on the long journey from rank beginner to excellence, is disingenuous. There's a chance

---

[7] Pliny attributes the moto to the painter Apelles, referring to his diligence: *Nulla dies sine linea* -- "Not a day without a line drawn."

they might be. But both statements trivialise effort and time invested. Any recommendation based on such a paper-thin foundation is questionable. If we're defining what to look for in a SCUBA instructor to teach cave diving, a recommendation from someone who's taken a course that probably lasted two or three days and may have been punctuated with rum drinks and sunscreen, is a low bar.

IS IT ABOUT AGENCY OR INSTRUCTOR?

Let's start the checklist for finding the perfect instructor for Sam by visiting a piece of delusional SCUBA diving logic; a false dichotomy, a hasty generalization, and a non-sequitur rolled into a neat package.

If we were to visit any online SCUBA forum, without searching too carefully, we'd find one thread or more debating whether or not finding good instruction is simply a case of signing up for classes with a specific agency; in most cases, a not-for-profit club based in North Florida.

Restricting the available choices to a simple black and white prospect – one agency above all others because you believe the rest of a long list of agencies are dive-industry dross – makes as much sense as using a chocolate teacup for a mid-morning cuppa. That Florida-based group are good, but they aren't selling silver bullets in a world filled with werewolves.

Mark Manson, the bestselling author of *The Subtle Art of Not Giving a F*ck*, points out there are a few arguments that really do have only two options. He writes, "I could say, 'There are two kinds of people in this world: people named Ron and people not named Ron.' This is a true dichotomy and a valid argument: you're either named Ron or you're not." But he goes on to explain that it's obviously wrong and invalid to say there are two kinds of people in the world: people named Ron and ****ing idiots. (His term.)

First of all, there are Rons out there who meet both criteria, and anyway, my name isn't Ron, and probably nor is yours, and since you've been enlightened enough to buy my book... well, enough said.

As a kid growing up within earshot of Millwall's Lion's Den, I heard this same flawed logic floating around the gloomy New Cross air every home-game Saturday: "Our team is the best! Everyone else is garbage!" This sort of chant is echoed by football supporters in every city in England... probably in the world. But the fact is that the home team – Millwall in particular – lose on a regular basis, some more than others. Millwall is not Liverpool FC by any measure.

The same can be true of a dive agency – every dive agency – werewolves or otherwise. People are involved in running agencies. There are variables. Ignoring that fact and its implications follows seriously dubious logic that breaks down eventually to a "You're either with us or against us", argument. And that argument in particular makes for a poor stating point from which to answer a question.

Beware the false dichotomy.

To be clear, I don't believe the agency is unimportant (I'm part owner of one), it's just the for a student like Sam, the agency she certifies through is a small part of a much larger expression on one side of a multi-factor equation[8]. So, let's look at what else there is.

FINDING THE PERFECT DANCE PARTNER FOR SAM

First, we should cover reputations and recommendations since they're a natural follow-on from the agency/instructor argument. Both reputation and recommendation are distillations of what others think of someone, rather than a deep investigation into that person's actual character, and the way they'll work for an individual – in this case, our hypothetical wanna-be cave diver. Reputation and recommendations – street creds – are not necessarily a bad starting point but treat them as a starting point at best. This is particularly true when searching for someone to teach an activity as difficult and life-affirming as playing a piano, free-climbing, paragliding, whitewater canoeing, or SCUBA diving of any sort; cave diving specifically.

Reputations are built on the shaky platform of three variables: personal interactions, second-hand interactions, and distant hearsay. One could argue that all three tend to be coloured with a bias of one sort or another. The woman who used to look after my dog when I was travelling regularly, had a reputation in the village as being 'weird'. When I asked for details, I was told she was a snob and distant and not very nice. When I mentioned her name, a server in the local diner told me that she was "difficult to talk to", but it turned out that server had never actually met her.

I hired the dog sitter regardless. It came to light she had earned the weirdness label because she was a cellist in the local

---

[8] And on the other hand, choosing which agency to partner with for dive shops and instructors, is a critically important business decision.

orchestra, her wife had died in a boating accident, and to help deal with the grief, she self-medicated with THC (legal here in Canada), and she preferred animals (horses in particular) to people. The perfect trifactor to generate gossip in my small rural cottage-country community.

The facts were different. My dog loved her, she was uber reliable, affordable, and friendly. When I moved to another part of the district, she gave me a signed CD of Baroque cello music, and a monster-sized package of organic dog treats! I gave the treats to the pup and kept the CD for myself.

So, beware the variables.

Recommendations should come with a disclaimer, too.

If I recommend a bespoke tailor to you, a man or woman to whom you're about to give five grand of your money, to make you a suit or a dress, you'd be wise to ask what I'm comparing them to? How many tailors have I used? How much bespoke clothing is hanging in my wardrobe? What's my recommendation based on?

Here's a thought to consider. With few exceptions, every diver who has recently purchased a closed-circuit rebreather (CCR, an advanced and expensive specialised piece of dive kit) recommends it to their friends. They assure anyone who'll listen, it's the greatest CCR they've every used; but it also happens to be the only CCR they've ever used. Couple that with the basic human reluctance to own up to any level of buyer's regret, especially when the sticker price of their purchase is three or four times the cost of bespoke tailoring. And therein lies the problem with recommendations.

Without an objective 360-degree search of the surroundings, recommendations can be hugely unreliable. Especially when given without being asked for. Your imaginary uncle, Sid the dentist brother of your imaginary father, might warn you off a specific brand of toothpaste. Not because of its lack of gingivitis-fighting abilities, but its taste. But you try it anyway and love the flavour: cinnamon.

People have different tastes. I like toothpaste that tastes like the warm pastries sold at early morning bakeries: apparently, imaginary uncle Sid does not. I also like smoked eel and *Weißbier*. My partner gags at the thought of either.

So, a good plan is to evaluate the veracity and value of any recommendation on your terms and your preferred taste. Both vary.

EXPECTATIONS AND EXPERIENCE

All that considered, in her bid to find the right instructor, Sam Diver needs to decide where she wants to get to, what the goal is, and how will she recognize it when she gets there? Tolkien wrote: "The road goes ever on and on down from the door where it began. Now far ahead the Road has gone, and I must follow, if I can".

A little allegorical perhaps, but not a bad summary of how long and complicated the flowchart describing what's available to a budding cave diver like Sam, who's decided to move on from the basics.

Without defined parameters, not only does the road go on and on, but the destination also becomes unpredictable. Similar to guessing the outcome of throwing two 12-sided gaming dice.

There are a staggering level of diving specialties, and as many different qualifications for divers and dive instructors. It's absolutely not one-size-fits-all. A class of experienced divers expecting to learn about the physiological impact of bailing out to 50/50 mix of oxygen and helium at 21 metres during the decompression phase of a rebreather dive that's gone pear-shaped, would be disappointed by a chat with a newly minted open-water instructor explaining the benefits of using baby shampoo as a mask defogger.

The experienced divers would expect to learn from a dive pro with a background in deep rebreather diving, who possessed the knowledge and qualifications to teach it. Both that person, and the person pushing the use of shampoo might be instructors... but that's not the same thing at all. And that incompatibility works both ways.

This is not a perfect compassion but let's say your cousin Carmalita wanted to learn basic accounting. Signing up with a specialist in differential equations and pre-calculus might not get them the best results possible. Certainly, any maths specialist would know simple addition and multiplication, and they may be engaged enough to take a swing at teaching your cousin the differences between single and double-entry bookkeeping, but the odds are they wouldn't be good at it, and poor Carmalita – and her clients – would be on their way to the deepest audit in history.

Using similar metrics, a classroom full of new divers would bail out and run away liked scared rabbits, if, when expecting to learn how to keep a SCUBA mask clear, were presented instead with a lecture on the vagaries of isobaric counter diffusion in deep trimix diving.

Beware the variables.

To cut down on those variables, Sam Diver has decided that her goal is to dive the Swiss Syphon Tunnel in Jailhouse Cenote, in

Tulum, QR Mexico. A place she has seen a photograph of and was thrilled by.

STYLE + CHEMISTRY

An instructor's style and the personal chemistry between them and their students is about character: who they really are rather than reputation or references. And all that is an important factor in the search criterion. My first SCUBA instructor was a character. He had a decidedly military outlook on life. A one-time member of the British parachute regiment, his teaching style was a cliché reflecting his background and mirroring that regiment's moto "Utringue Paratus" (ready for anything). The class was challenging (think: Fight Club but with water); the academics, sparse ("read the book until you know what's in it, so you don't bother me by asking questions"); the in-water skills development, well-defined, but scary ("if you don't do what I tell you to do, you will die")!

He was a true dinosaur, his approach, teaching philosophy, and distribution of empathy emanated from the Tomás de Torquemada school of human relations. Hopefully, we will never see his like again.

However, the members of that historical BSAC class loved him. And there are people still who thrive on a level of harshness in their life, and although doubtful that an individual as rough and ready as that would last more than one class teaching for any major SCUBA agency today, his class was epic, memorable, and effective.

There are instructors who still represent a similar, if slightly less extreme, outlook on their job. These folks represent the extreme end of the SCUBA -instructor spectrum. My suggestion would be to avoid them. Their brutal honesty is an acquired taste, and too strong for today's average consumer.

Thankfully, the majority of instructors are closer to the other end of that spectrum since most students respond better to learning in a less stressful environment. The best way for Sam Diver to tell what she's getting is meeting her instructor face-to-face.

Given all the other prerequisites for an instructor – the appropriate experience and qualifications, a match to the student's expectations, location of their courses, and so on – taking the time to find someone whose style suits, and whose chemistry is compatible is key to success. The dive industry does not collect data from people who try diving, earn their basic certification, and then rarely or never dive again. We should. It's a good metric to show customer satisfaction and how good a job everybody did matching up a student to the right instructor... and vice versa!

In our case, with our hypothetical diver looking for a hypothetical cave instructor, a personal interview – actual, not hypothetical – is a must. Video conference, fine; actual conference, preferred. And among the bank of questions that Sam Diver need answers to are ones where the potential instructor explains why he or she cave dives. Their reasons should be poetic and make Sam excited to try it herself.

THE QUALIFICATIONS YOU NEED

Which brings us to qualifications and what to look for. Oh, and to be clear, this section is about our hypothetical student diver's qualifications, not the instructor's.

Working as a cave instructor was an absolute pleasure. They were remarkable years. But it was hard work, a little frustrating occasionally, and scary at times, and I miss none of that. I just miss things that are hard to explain but cool. A year or so after I'd chucked it in, a close friend asked me what I missed most. I threw off some hogwash, gibberish; a random answer about the physical challenge of pushing students to the edge of their comfort zone, and the mental stimulation of thinking faster than Murphy so that I had a few seconds warning before things went pear-shaped. Pseudo-intellectual, forebrain-generated smokescreen stuff that actually hides what cave diving and teaching it is really about.

When Zen practitioners meditate, they strive for a state of mind they call Hishiryo (Before Thinking). The way I understand it, hishiryo is that brief moment you look at something, know precisely what it is, exactly how it fits into its surroundings, everything it does, and how it relates and connects to you, all before your mind tells you what it is; before you put a label on it. Well, in a strange way, that is exactly what cave diving is about. And what's abundantly cool about being a cave instructor is turning students on to that experience.

It's the moment of 'enlightenment' when after all the work and struggle, all the object lessons wrapped in little failures, and all the embarrassing and disorienting moments, your student finally swims into a new passageway with grace and looking like they belong, and you hear them catch their breath, see their body language change in a subtle, barely noticeable way, and know they have just experienced a moment of hishiryo.

I miss that.

So, how does that relate to the skills Sam needs to make her cave instruction gel? A willingness to forget most of what she already knows about diving, a mind like a sponge or the classic Zen empty teacup, and an ability that scientists, like Ellen Winner, call 'self-regulatory behaviour'.

It's Sam's ability to understand and manage her behaviour and her reactions, to feelings and things happening around her, with grace and calmness. It includes her being able to regulate reactions to strong emotions like frustration, excitement, anger, and embarrassment. And also, to maintain an internal balance regardless of the pressure from external pressures.

We could boil this down to a very simple test... if Sam spends any time suffering from road rage, the stresses of cave diving might be too much for her!

HELP FOR SAM DIVER... and anyone else who needs it.

This chapter rambles but let's settle on it being how to find help. Here are some pointers in no particular order, which probably makes the rest of this chapter superfluous.

1) It's unlikely that your open water instructor is actually a genius. The best we can hope for is competency.

2) It's equally unlikely that you are a natural diver. The best we can hope for is being comfortable in the water with a significant percentage of your bodyweight in dive gear strapped to you.

3) The secret to one and two is practice. Talent helps but work trumps all.

4) There are more than 120 agencies issuing certification for SCUBA divers. Picking which one is best will probably take you down a long and winding path. Don't bother unless you are a masochist or are partial to conspiracy theories.

5) Chose a goal... someplace you want to visit. For this exercise I chose a specific cave that is particularly beautiful; one of many in that area. I'm biased, but this book is about cave diving, so my choice is apt.

6) Look for an instructor you feel comfortable with, with whom you have chemistry, who dives what you want to dive. Speak to them. Listen to them. It's good if they are poetically enthusiastic, experienced, empathetic.

7) Reputation and recommendations are worth their weight in something extremely light.

8) Be prepared to learn. Cave diving is about that but learn without letting thoughts get in the way. You'll pick it up faster that way.

Question Eleven

DO CAVE DIVERS HAVE A DEATH WISH? WHAT ON EARTH IS WORTH RISKING YOUR LIFE FOR IN A CAVE? YOU PEOPLE ARE NUTS. YOU'D NEVER CATCH ME DOING THAT... AND SO ON.

- When I was spending a good portion of my year cave diving in North Florida, there were times when I regretted wearing a target on my back: having Canadian plates on my vehicle. People in the parking lot at my hotel, at Winn Dixie, or the local BBQ joint, trying to be polite and make conversation, would ask, "What brings you to Florida?" Most of the time I'd explain I was a cave diver, and we'd chat, since that was seldom the expected answer. Naturally, comments varied. Most were happy to show interest, but others felt it necessary to insult my choices by letting me know they thought I was crazy and an idiot. One woman explained she was a school trustee – nice, but never understood the implications – and she believed all the caves in Florida should be closed because "...the devil lives in them, and cave divers are ungodly heathens who worship Satan". I try never to argue. Florida residents may carry a gun without a permit, so I try awfully hard never to argue. But sometimes a slowball comes down the middle of the plate, and it would be foolish not to take a swing.

Statistics is a branch of mathematics I actually enjoy. Statistics is a science with the most... what's the word? Slop. That's it. Statistics is unruly. Most sciences sit nicely in their seat without fidgeting. Physics, chemistry, biology, paleontology might fidget a little, but you always know roughly where to look in the classroom to find the well-behaved and trusty sciences. But not so with statistics. Statistics is as likely to be hanging from the closet door or be hidden inside the closet as it is to be seated quietly. Stats cannot be trusted. I love statistics!

There's the famous saying from Mark Twain about statistics that must be one of the most quoted lines in the English language, but I much prefer George Canning's observation: "I can prove anything by statistics except the truth". Same message but in a different wrapper. And while I totally agree with Twain and Canning – a 19th century British statesman and short-term prime minister, by the way – I feel the urge to share a few statistics about dangerous activities.

The British Medical Journal, analysing stats from Canada's west coast which reported equestrian injuries over a five-year period, concluded that – using admission to hospital as the benchmark (since it would indicate more serious injury than a visit to the emergency department) – horse riding is more dangerous than either skiing or motorcycling.

I have some personal experience in this regard. As a young man, I fell off my share of motorcycles and horses. If I had any street creds at all, it was that I would fall off a sofa given enough time. And now, as a much older man, I still fall off telemark skis occasionally. People die doing all three of these activities. So, there's no disagreement, they are potentially dangerous (so is golf, ten-pin bowling, and spending too long under a sunlamp). But really, horse-riding is top of that list of risky activities. Ah, yes; statistics at work.

There's more.

A US-based insurance company recently published a very attractive infographic online, ranking dangerous sports in order of insurance category. Assessed risk (defined by type of injury) was indicated by icons in the shape of tiny white skulls, one through six. Parachuting, skydiving, paragliding, and hang-gliding each earn six skulls, while something labelled 'holiday activities' ranked one. Scuba diving (which I take to be simple recreational SCUBA: reefs, colourful fishes, tropical, clear, water), was in the one skull category. Cave diving was credited with five, along with bull riding, rock climbing, and white-water rafting. Base jumping and heli-skiing where both off the scale and had six white skulls plus one red one.

Ah, more statistics, and although the graphic listed where the data for its rankings were pulled from, George and Mark would be happy to see that nothing about statistics has changed since their time. My opinion is these insurance company stats are shockingly simple-minded and peppered with baseless assumptions. Let me try to explain.

Perhaps, first I should declare a conflict of interest. Since I started cave diving, and especially when I began to teach cave diving and Closed-Circuit Rebreather diving, I have had such a hard job finding affordable personal insurance through regular channels, that I gave up long ago. So, maybe I am biased and conflicted about insurance companies. Best to factor that into any assessment you make of my reasoning and rationale!

Just to be perfectly clear, cave divers do not have a death wish. More to the point, most of them are perfectly sane, and don't plan on dying; not in a cave or anywhere else for at least 50 years. If there's a single thing driving someone to cave dive it's not some aberrant wish to cheat death, it's something else. Discipline perhaps: the process of planning dives and their careful and detailed execution. Discipline is high on the list when one troubles to ask.

I cannot speak for the training that bull riders work through, but I have 'done' rock climbing and white-water rafting, and cave diving has a very, very different lead time. And although there's no bull riding in my past, I feel comfortable writing that the workup to become a cave diver is an order of magnitude more complicated than sticking a cowboy hat on your head, screaming "Yippee-Ki-Yay, Mother******!" and holding on 'real tight!'.

WHAT A CAVE CLASS INCLUDES

Let's take as read that someone signed up for a cave diving class is already an experienced diver and therefore understands risk and its management. Since risk is a topic covered at every level of diver training, from day one, this is a valid assumption.

As a starting point down this road, we can condense that the golden rule of risk management taught to any diver is: Follow the rules, dive within their experience (what they've done lately, not what they were doing a couple of years ago), dive within the limits of their training, don't dive alone. There's more to it than this, but it's a good start, and covers the basic process taught to beginners.

So, given all the above, a cave diving class takes around a week, perhaps a day or two longer. There will be many hours of diving and learning skills, hands-on demonstrations, and role-playing. And this is the part cave instructors (and to be clear, cave diving instructors are at the top of their game), love about teaching the class, but before getting into the water, class begins on day one with a module on accident analysis.

Accident analysis is a detailed look at cave-diving deaths, what happened, what seems to have caused them, and what we can learn from them. The analysis can be disturbing. One reason for including this rather grim segment in cave courses is to underscore the gravity and responsibility that cave diving demands. There's no bravado, just reality.

When I was teaching cave diving, I had one student leave the class after this module. Turns out he was being pressured by his partner to take the class, and talking about death and dying tipped the balance in favour of him bailing out. "It's not for me", is the edited version of his reason to quit early. He earned my respect, but his partner was peeved. I suggested he leave too, and he did.

Students learn during this analysis that few of these cave deaths are accidents. Much more often they are the result of people bending or breaking the rules; either exceeding the limits of their training or failing to follow established protocols taught in cave diving classes. Accidents themselves – distinct from misadventures leading to something hitting the fan – are extremely rare.

A SAD EXAMPLE

I'm not in the habit of issuing warnings about what I write, and I think the qualifications given by BBC announcers that some listeners may find what follows disturbing, are overwrought, but what follows may be disturbing. If you're sensitive to these things, please skip to the end of this chapter.

The hardest part of picking apart any mishaps for accident analysis is sorting through hearsay and shabby evidence to get to what matters, and what people need to be told. However, sometimes an episode is so clearly sad and based on such unambiguously wrong-headed decisions, that its stands as a well-defined, hard-edged, black and white example of sheer madness. This is one of those cases and there can be little doubt what went wrong, and where responsibilities for those deaths **lie**.

Darrin Spivey bought his son, Dillon Sanchez, a set of double SCUBA tanks for Christmas that year (this was 2013). Double SCUBA tanks are favoured by technical divers especially for deep dives and cave dives, because double tanks are often larger than standard SCUBA cylinders, and since there are two of them, they hold a lot of gas. Another reason technical divers opt to use doubles of the type Spivey gave his son, is they are configured in such a way that in the event of a leak or the failure of a regulator – uncommon but possible – there are several options to manage the event, and for the diver to make it home safely.

Because doubles are many postal codes away from the standard kit commonly used by 15-year-old divers – and yes,

Sanchez was only 15 when he died – the strong recommendation within the SCUBA diving community is that divers take specific training to learn how to operate doubles safely and competently. It's also generally recommended the student is 18 or older.

During that training – usually a couple of days spent with a specialist technical diving instructor – the focus is on weighting and trim, shutdown drills (what to do in the event of a failure or leak of some kind), buoyancy adjustments (doubles require a special buoyancy device since they are heavy), and pre-and post-dive checks and procedures. To a non-diver, someone unfamiliar with technical dive gear, this must sound like gobbledegook, but key here is that this type of training and mentorship is complicated and well beyond the scope of anything a regular diver would need using standard open-water SCUBA diving gear. For the record, doubles and their setup and use are well beyond anything the average diving instructor is 'licenced' to teach. Doubles (AKA a twinset) are highly specialized equipment.

Simply put, doubles – and the extra 'bits and pieces' of non-standard gear required to use them in the water – take some getting used to and are not a trivial departure from the SCUBA diving norm. Also, I'm not sure how strong Dillon Sanchez was, but most 15-year-olds would struggle to properly manage doubles in and out of the water. They are bulky, they are heavy, and they can be difficult to swim with comfortably.

If you ride horses, an analogy that might help to illustrate this point is that doubles are to regular SCUBA gear, what riding point-to-point on a feisty warmblood show jumper is to a five-year-old enjoying a sedate Shetland pony ride on the beach at Camber Sands.

That said, it's worth considering in all this, that Sanchez did not have this training. In fact, the young man had no formal SCUBA training of any kind and wasn't a certified diver at any level at all. This is an important detail, and we'll come back to it, but right now, a little information about the dive site where he and his father died.

The Eagles Nest is in the Chassahowitzka National Wildlife Refuge. It's well off the beaten path, totally isolated, and surrounded by Florida swamp and brush. Access is via a dirt road and, although I once made the 20-minute journey from the state highway in a small car, is best done in a truck with good ground clearance and four-wheel drive. Consequently, this is not a site that attracts casual passers-by; diving at the Eagles Nest signifies there was definite intent and prior planning.

I have dived there many times. My first visit was under the watchful eye of a Florida-based cave diving instructor-trainer named Larry Green. This was in the early spring of 1994 and at that time, access to the site was controlled, and Larry was one of the few people who had permission to dive there, and a key to unlock a gate blocking the access road. For the record, when Larry guided me, I had logged more than a couple of thousand dives, more than 120 of them in caves. I was a certified technical instructor trainer, and a member of the training advisory panel for a leading certification agency. In short, I met the suggested prerequisites to enter this complex underwater cave system. But nevertheless, my first dive at Eagles Nest was a challenge.

Like many extensive caves, on the surface, Eagles Nest is unimpressive; just a murky little water hole in the middle of scrub, saw palmetto, and stands of Florida pine and live oak. Once below this muddy pond's surface, visibility is usually very poor until one enters the cave proper (perhaps less than a metre). Therefore, one follows a thin line – this line is usually 5mm white nylon kernmantle, the traditional permanent line installed in most Florida caves. A diver would follow this line for several minutes to arrive at a large, submerged tree trunk in about 6 metres of water. From there, they would follow the same line to enter the cave via one of two vertical, almost perfectly cylindrical chimneys.

The larger of these (the entrance) is just about big enough for two (in moderate comfort) or maybe three divers in full kit to fit through in cramped conditions. However, after dropping a few metres deeper, divers enter 'the ballroom', which is a huge underwater gallery the size of a hockey arena. It is remarkable, truly a wonderful piece of natural beauty.

The line that the divers have followed since submerging, now drops straight down to the top of a pile of rubble (the debris from the collapse of the roof forming the two chimneys above). At this point, the divers would be at around 38 metres or 125 feet, and here the line splits into two, each line disappearing into either the upstream or downstream tunnels, both of which extend for many hundreds of metres, reaching depths of 90 metres (about 300 feet). At times these tunnels are massive, and at others, the walls, floor and ceiling bite down into quite challenging restrictions. However, all in all, Eagles Nest is a beautiful and impressive example of the experience the Florida Karst offers qualified, and responsible, certified cave divers. And cave divers from around the world do visit this site. As such, it and the many other popular caves in North Florida, provide a considerable economic boost to the region, and several local small businesses depend on the adventure tourism market.

Now, let's return to Spivey and his son.

I never met with Spivey or any of his family, but following this tragedy on Boxing Day 2013, his family said that he was careful and not given to risky behaviour. If we choose to question the veracity of this statement – and we should if we are serious about analyzing the incident in which he and his son perished – all we can do is look at his actions through the lens of hindsight.

What does hindsight uncover? Spivey was a certified diver. But his certification fell far short of being a certified cave diver, and there is a huge gap between his certification and what he needed to make a dive at Eagles Nest Sink. To use our horse-riding analogy once more, one does not jump on a thoroughbred and try to ride the Kentucky Derby, straight after learning to canter at the local riding school. In essence, this is what the 35-year-old father was attempting to do.

Word is that he had one friend who was cave certified, and on several occasions, pressed Spivey to take at least a basic-level cave diving course. He chose to ignore this advice.

During the certification course he did take – a basic SCUBA diving class qualifying him to dive with a similarly certified buddy to a maximum depth of something between 18-20 metres, depending on the agency he certified through – Spivey would have been told by his instructor, and would have read in his student workbook, that venturing into an overhead environment (such as a cave, a cavern, inside a shipwreck, etc.) is well beyond the scope of the training he was taking (the very basic beginner's class). That warning is part of every reputable training agency's basic curriculum. It is mandated by the various industry associations whose task it is to set community-wide training standards. He would have been reminded of this by a large sign between the parking area and the water's edge at Eagles Nest. That sign warns divers that the site is a complex one, demanding specialized equipment and training. Spivey chose to ignore this advice.

Also, during his certification course, Spivey would have learned that 'teaching' a friend or family member to SCUBA dive – even in a swimming pool – is frowned upon, because the possibility of inflicting serious, life-changing injury, even death, is possible. Yes, even in a swimming pool, death is possible. Spivey chose to ignore this advice.

One of many pieces of additional knowledge he would have also picked up during his training, was that when you try out new gear, the best practice is to do so in safe, benign conditions: a swimming pool, a shallow ocean bay with little or no current, a quarry, a quiet arm of a lake. Spivey chose to ignore this advice too. Even more questionable, he took his son to try out unfamiliar gear to a complex, highly technical cave that – once entered – presented that boy with a sheer drop of more than 30 metres in a pitch-black, very spooky environment.

The bare facts are that he took his son, uncertified, untrained, perhaps unaware of the risks, to a dive site that is considered one of the most challenging in that part of Florida, to try new, complex, and specialized gear, which would have been unfamiliar to him. These are not the actions of someone who was as careful and adverse to risky behaviour as his family believed he was.

My opinion was at the time of the incident, Spivey's behaviour was deplorable. In my opinion, Spivey was a classic example of the Dunning-Kruger Effect and the Normalization of Deviance, both oversights being dangerous and foolhardy. In essence, his actions indicate that he probably thought he was hot stuff, and he believed the rules did not apply to him. He was wrong. He was not qualified to dive any cave, and certainly not one as challenging as Eagles Nest. Unfortunately, he paid for his monumental error of judgement with his life. The saddest thing is that he dragged his son along with him, and that young man paid the same price, "...for the sins of his father". They both ran out of air and drowned. All indications are that the boy died first, his father later.

Spivey's family called for the Eagles Nest site to be closed, "to prevent further tragedy".

Cave diving carries risk – proper training, the right equipment serviced and appropriately used, building experience slowly by following the established instructional pathway, and carefully planning dives well within personal limits – greatly mitigates that risk, but can never remove it entirely. Therefore, cave diving and diving in general is a risky endeavour. But then again, so is horse riding, snowmobiling, downhill skiing, mountain biking, playing rugby, and so on. The list of outdoor activities that carry a degree of risk is long and growing every week. Worth noting, too, is that people have died playing golf. Yet, there are no documented instances I can find in the literature of back-country trails, ski hills, rugby grounds, or golf courses being closed to prevent further tragedy.

Any call to close the Eagles Nest – or any cave based on the Spivey/Sanchez incident – is a red herring argument, since it does not address the primary issues: in this case, extremely poor judgement (going against reasoned advice) and a disgraceful attitude towards risk (believing that 'it will not happen to me'). Spivey was not typical of the cave-diving community; just the opposite. His behaviour was aberrant: contrary to everything taught and promoted within our community, and by its leadership. His misadventures, in fact, have nothing at all to do with the activity of cave diving, since he had not earned a place in that community, and he defied every rule, every best practice, and every safeguard we include in any training.

I have been careful not to refer to the Boxing Day 2013 incident as an accident because an accident is, "...an event that happens by chance or that is without apparent or deliberate cause". That does not apply to any part of this 'event.' This was an outrageous, flagrant, and shocking example of diver ignorance and foolishness.

THE TROUBLE WITH THE STATISTICS

It seems clear – at least in my opinion – that the cause of these two deaths has very little, if anything, to do with the environment or the sport of responsible cave diving. Rather, it has lots to do with Spivey's actions and his total disregard for the rules. Is it correct then to include this particular disaster as part of any list of cave diving accidents?

If that's the case, then what about the other times that people have gone into a cave without the training, equipment, or experience? Is it fair to paint them as cave diving accidents, or do we need to have an ancillary one entitled 'death by poor judgement'? Occasionally, people have died in caves because they have been told by a friend that it'll be okay to just look inside. It wasn't, and they paid a very high price to find that out. Almost always, the people who die in caves had no business being there. Should this be classified as 'death by Darwin'? I'm not sure, but I simply wish that people would stay out of caves and follow the rules... they're not a secret.

There's no question that SCUBA diving is dangerous. Cave diving is dangerous. So is crossing Oxford Street or Fifth Avenue or Bloor Street et al during the week before Christmas or the days leading up to Lunar New Year.

I can't speak for every responsible diver – every cave diver – but those I know well feel exactly as I do: the risk takers, those divers who push limits without regard for the consequences, the reckless and thoughtless, the cowboys and careless, the gamblers and short-odds-players, do our sport a grave injustice. It's probably fair to say that the real technical diving community – from seasoned explorers to the newly-minted cavern diver – would vote unanimously to disown them.

All diving, whether simple sport diving or the most elaborate technical diving, entails risk. As divers, we accept that, otherwise we would never strap several kilos of dive gear to our body before jumping into water too deep to stand in.

A good friend, a true explorer, a woman who has travelled to places underwater where fewer than a handful of people have been, admits she feels fear. She says that being scared is normal, and the day that feeling isn't there, she will hang up her fins. She explains being frightened is what drives us to plan our dives so meticulously; our fears lessen as we go through our pre-dive checks and drills. So, when it's time to get into the water, the fear is replaced by excitement, and the reassurance that we have done what we can to mitigate the risk.

We mitigate risk by following a proven risk-management process. We identify the risks; measure how likely they are to present themselves during our dives and evaluate their potential impact; we examine possible solutions based on personal experience, our training, and proven best practices (nothing's made up on the fly). All that done, we implement the solution or solutions that best fit our needs, and finally, we monitor the results. Next time around, we adjust things informed by what we learned on previous dives.

It's a simple but effective strategy, and we're shown it and how to use it from our very first SCUBA lesson. As our training and experience grows, so too does the depth and scope of our risk-management planning. Nothing is left to chance. Well, that's a silly thing to say because there is always a chance that the unplanned-for happens. Well-experienced divers and well-planned dives very occasionally go seriously off the rails. That is inevitable yet acceptable to us given the benefits and sheer joys of cave diving.

Caves offer those who chose to swim in them, a true challenge. The training can be arduous, the equipment is expensive, the learning curve long and non-lineal.

And caves are also self-policing. What I mean by that is the caves themselves tend to weed out the cowboys and cavaliers. Those whose approach to technical diving generally – and cave diving specifically – is lax and uninformed; those who don't have the appropriate training; those wearing the wrong gear, and those whose dive plans aren't informed by actual cave-diving experience. These folks may have a 'come-to-Jesus' moment during their dive. They may run low on gas. They may not remember which tunnel is the way out of the cave. They may brush a fin against a mound of silt so fine that all visibility disappears in a dark grey cloud. Their light may give up the ghost, and they experience a dark deeper than any other.

And at that time, they come face-to-face in real-time with their own mortality. Not on a screen in a video game, not remotely like during a movie, not pretending and playing games with an easy out. But with their heart hammering noisily against their ribs, and the strange and unwelcome taste of bile and iron rising in their throat.

For a few, the outcome is not something to chat about blithely: X-rated for horror as with Spivey. Best we leave it there. For most, the extent of the 'policing exercise' is less final than that, and they make it back to the surface. Their nasty experience may come on their first gamble, it may come on their twenty-first, but it will come. And when it does, the sensible ones hang up their fins. The others skew the statistics.

So, to wrap this up, I invited the Florida school trustee woman to research the Normalization of Deviance, the Dunning-Kruger effect, and to read the various online and printed articles dealing with accident analysis. I mentioned she could read some of the books published on cave diving and safety. I told her she'd find no mention of Satan. I resisted telling her she was a sad, misguided woman who should take the bible out of her arse and read it in the hope of learning something. However, I did tell her she needed professional help.

She told me to ****-off.

So much for the Christian virtues of peace, love, and understanding.

Question Twelve

IS THERE AN AGE LIMIT FOR CAVE DIVING?

- When I used to attend family functions – a broken habit now – there was always someone, an aunt, an in-law, a dodgy distant cousin from the side of the family tree in need of severe pruning – who would ask, "Are you still doing your diving thing?" This question, inevitable and as constant as the northern star, always focused on age rather than ability. The frequency of this type of personal inquiry, and the questioner's surprise at my positive replies, greatly increased as my hair and beard became whiter and whiter. In fact, as this book was being prepared for the publisher, I was asked again, when I would 'give it up?', but this time it was from a fellow cave diver who is of similar vintage, and who was getting ready to dive a wiggly, highly decorated cave south of Chunyaxché, Mexico. We discussed things and decided to carry on until we get it

right, or until our wheelchairs get irreparably tangled in
our dive gear.

Epigenetics: I wonder if that is still a dirty word in medical circles. In
fact, I wonder if it was ever a dirty word? An old friend explained
epigenetics to me a decade ago and finished off her explanation by
saying it's all hogwash, totally bloody hogwash. I was cooking and
drinking wine at the time, so what went on between my initial
question – what's epigenetics? – and the hogwash comment, may be
misremembered, but I was a big fan of the concept: hogwash
notwithstanding. Still am.

My friend, a doctor, the regular kind rather than someone
who's successfully defended a thesis entitled, "Hidden themes of the
mid-20th century reactionary Catholic movement to be found in
Tintin cartoons". She explained that epigenetics was "...where
pseudo-science meets the Saturday lifestyle section in the Toronto
Star". She said the argument that one's genes are the cards in a hand
of bridge or canaster or whatever someone is dealt with at birth, and
epigenetics is how that person plays that hand in life, "...makes
sense if we're talking about fungus or stingrays, but it doesn't work
for people". I remember she was quite adamant and a little drunk,
and her partner lead her out of the kitchen with a backwards glance
as if to say, 'for god's sake, man, don't get her started...'

I've not really followed up since and haven't asked any other
medical folk for their opinions on the topic. I am still a little shy
about stirring up another hornet's nest. However, the idea that we
can influence whichever one of the Fates wields the scissors, by
eating right, indulging in physical activity, not smoking, cutting out
wayward alcohol consumption, and staying away from the daytime
smog polluting the streets of New Delhi and the like, is appealing.

Moreover, supporting the concept may have a placebo effect, and trick time sufficiently well to stave off the inevitable day when fins, cylinders, regulators and drysuits get shoved in the back of the storage unit.

To some extent, one has to be a little lucky to have the energy and drive to keep diving when the convention play shuffleboard and bingo. And as annoying as my family's silly questions were, they were well meant. Unfortunately thought, close to impossible to answer. There is really no prescribed age limit or fitness level beyond the rather vague, if it feels good, keep at it. To an extent, it's self-policing. Certainly, some have an easier time than others feeling good (the genetic lottery), and some make the most of the hand they're dealt (the quasi-science of epigenetics).

ADVICE FROM THE MEDICAL PROFESSION

Frankly, any notions I have about 'The Aging Diver' come from Google and two experts: Dan Orr and David Carash. Dan is president emeritus of Divers Alert Network, an organisation he ran for more than 20 years. David is a board-certified emergency medicine, undersea and hyperbaric medicine physician.

Charash has developed workshops, symposiums, lectures, and hosts a podcast (Fitness in Diving), which is a wonderful resource for any diver. Dan is a regular guest with stellar street cred. To the point where a new, younger diver, once explained to me that Dan "invented oxygen".

That aside, both are divers and both abundantly qualify as authorities on maintaining the diving habit as one ages, through career choices and, forgive me guys, personal experience.

The best advice possible to give is to check them out.

Aside from that, one of the basic pieces of advice to every diver, young, old, or in-between, is to drink lots of fluid. Dive lore has it that being well hydrated helps manage the threat of decompression stress, and muscle performance. Dive medicine informs that older adults exhibit decreased thirst sensation and reduced fluid intake.

And for the record, knocking back a litre of water on the way to the dive site is ineffective. It just makes peeing inevitable. Hydration means maintaining a three-litre a day habit, especially on multiday dive excursions.

IT'S DIFFERENT FOR DIVE PROS

There are guidelines for instructors to follow which are published by that instructor's governing agency. Annual checkups and medical signoffs need to be filed when membership is renewed. Some agencies are more focused on this than others, but as you can imagine, there are some potential legal and civil actions that could result from an agency suspending any member they suspect of being unfit. But occasionally it happens.

One issue is what constitutes observable signs. It's not as simple as noticing that a member is overweight, smokes cigars while teaching, has a bottle of 15-year-old single malt and a Glencairn whisky glass beside them in the classroom, and tucks into a family-sized bag of Cheetos while lecturing. If there is an issue, it's often more subtle.

So, how fit does someone have to be to dive in a cave?

There's no question that cave diving is not as easy of falling off the back of a boat into clear, lukewarm water with a single aluminum SCUBA cylinder on one's back, to then hang semi-motionless while slowly drifting over a coral garden. That is the essence of SCUBA diving for the vast majority of certified divers. Scuba is part of their vacation plans, and although they may dive fewer than 20 times a year, these folks are the core of the recreational diving community. For them, diving is pure fun. Relatively simply, it's something to enjoy and to be proud of. For the record, a published average calorie burn is around 300/hr for this type of dive. Three dives a day, is a piece of cake... with ice-cream and chocolate shavings.

A cave dive demands more active participation. First there's getting the gear to the dive site. At many of the tourist caves, this can involve nothing more than a 10 metre walk from the car park to the water's edge; but it may also demand a few hundred metres of schlepping kit through the jungle on a trail that looks like a hamster run and is as equally difficult to navigate.

After cylinders – around 13 kilos each if we're using the most common type and plural since there would be a minimum of two, either individual for sidemount or twinned as a set of manifolded doubles and therefore bolted together – next is getting the lights, pouches, reels and spools, spare masks, odds and ends, and a drysuit or wetsuit comfortably situated. Then it's time to start swimming. (As an aside, I once weighed the equipment package for a double stage dive [four cylinders] to the backend of a cave in Florida, including backups, lights, drysuit, thermal underwear, survey slates, and various sundries. The whole package was almost one and a quarter times my body weight.)

And while the apparent weight of SCUBA gear is greatly reduced when it's lowered into water (even fresh water), its mass is unaffected, and that means there's still its inertia, the diver's weight, and water resistance itself to overcome. It takes effort to move it and yourself through the water, and while the average recreational diver uses around 300 calories on a one-hour dive, the average cave diver, in a low-flow cave, is burning three times that, according to a brief online search, several articles on diving generally, and personal 'finger in the wind' experience!

The calorie count is so high because cave divers swim – both ways if all goes well–and using the example of a typical dive in a shallow Mexican cave, an average diver will cover 15 metres a minute. Couple that with a normal starting volume of gas, and following all the standard limits, a two-hour dive is possible. That's works out to something approaching 900 metres each way.

WHY CAVE DIVERS EAT TACOS

Swimming 1800 metres covered in SCUBA gear, and pushing it through water, is a workout. But that would be a completely normal cave dive and similar to dozens or scores of dives being logged daily by members of the caving community. Clearly, dives in that league demand fairly robust cardiovascular fitness.

It's common practice to allow the fitness question to be answered by individuals – both instructors and students – without much in the way of oversight. While the process lacks accountability or an unbiased reference to an external authority, the community seems to function reasonably well, regardless. However, in the list of contributing factors to cave diving's 'bad trips', unconsidered health issues are a growing factor as the community ages... which it does.

HOW TO PREPARE FOR CAVE DIVING

The single best exercise is to swim. I live in an area of the world very light on municipal swimming pools, but heavy on freshwater lakes. For a few months, swimming in them is a joy. However, for a good portion of the year, comfort dictates wearing a wetsuit or cross-country skiing on their solid, frozen surface.

Bike riding is useful, so too are lifting weights and walking. If you need incentive, I can recommend getting a giant breed dog to get you into the habit of logging an hour or so of outdoor exercise every day... rain or shine! That I know of, there is no form of physical exercise that's bad for a cave diver except anything that damages the knees. Runners beware.

MENTAL FITNESS

The legendary Wayland Rhys Morgan explained that for a cave diver, there are three types of fitness to worry about: physical, because the gear is heavy; financial, because that's a heavy burden; and mental, since that's the heaviest burden of all. One issue with Morgan's advice was that every time he gave it, the percentages would be mixed up and the totals always added up to more than one hundred.

Another issue is that unless one has a personal therapist plugged into one's head on a semi-daily basis, how does one recognise the correct mental attitude is there to go cave diving?

And that is so purely personal, I'm not going there. All I can say is if it doesn't make you smile, stop doing it.

THE LAST WORD

So, from this, can we assume that to cave dive one has to be young? Is 40 over the hill for a cave diver? If someone is closer to retirement than grade school, should they forget about signing up for a cave diver class?

According to my family at the beginning of this tale, the answer appears to be, YES. Moreover, taking a look around the cenotes here in Mexico, the majority of the men and women who are teaching and receiving cave classes are 30-something.

It's enough to make one feel old. Perhaps it's time to wish for immortality.

THE GILGAMESH PROJECT

What brought this to mind recently was revisiting Yuval Noah Harari's book *Sapiens: A Brief History of Humankind*, and his reference to something called The Gilgamesh Project.

He describes the project as efforts to solve the "technical problem" of death. A situation in which medical science can push homo sapiens across an evolutionary threshold where immortality is possible.

The stuff of science-fiction? Certainly, it has a sci-fi ring to it. Sci-fi spiced with a little conspiracy theory if one reads between the lines in most of the literature on the topic. But the argument is that science has already extended life expectancy, and limited child mortality. The next step is to create a 'bionic immune system made up of nanobots that open blocked arteries and fight bacteria and cancer cells.'

While it seems reasonable to buy into epigenetics, following Gilgamesh, the King of Uruk, on a long and imagined journey to the underworld to discover the secret of immortality, is surely the stuff of nightmares.

However, all that taken into consideration, one is reminded of the music metric: 'If it's too loud, you're too old.' Slightly modified for current purposes: 'If you think you're too old, you are. Try golf.

Question Thirteen

"WHY DID YOU WRITE THAT THE RULE OF THIRDS ISN'T FIT FOR PURPOSE IN CAVE DIVING BECAUSE IT DOESN'T GUARANTEE SAFETY, IT JUST MAKES THE BODY RECOVERY EASIER?"

I worked for a while as editor for a chain of community newspapers in a beautiful region of Canada: trees, moose, two-billion-year-old rock, and freshwater lakes. Not much of global interest happened there, but I learned plenty of things that working for newspapers and magazines in London and Toronto do not teach. For example, newspaper copy in a rural, summer-cottage community has little use for off-hand references to Kafka, Molière or Octavio Paz, but a catchy headline is like a lamb shank to a lion. Years later, I used that knowledge writing a piece for an underwater magazine. The title created a little flutter. In hindsight maybe it was a mite too 'graphic.' You judge.

Standing up for the status quo is safe, but uncreative. In the 'Illustrated Encyclopaedia of Unexciting Ways to Live', the picture beside the listing for Status Quo it is a sepia-toned photo taken inside a Private Member's Club in London. It's the type of place with over-stuffed leather chairs, cigar smoke filling the air, and exotic animal heads hanging on the walls. The type of place that's so fixed in its ways that its most innovative act was to finally allow women to visit – but not to be members – at the turn of the 21st century. The picture tells all: Empire, stiff upper lip, palm trees, a cup of Darjeeling on the terrace, and 'Damn Everything Resembling Change'!

Considering all that, safe is the wrong word. Let's try stifling and uncreative. Certainly barren.

Change for the sake of nothing more than shaking up the status quo is not always the better option; but when directed at improving a process, baffling retrogression and misogyny, opening minds to opportunity and inclusiveness (or thinking laterally and more effectively), it is.

Essentially, accepting change often results in doing what works right now, as opposed to accepting the status quo solely because 'it's what we have always done'.

And all of that reasoning was behind titling a magazine article: *Is it time to rethink The Rule of Thirds?* With its opening sentence mentioning body recoveries and so on.

Since the intention here is not to teach a gas management class, I'll try to avoid falling down a rabbit hole brimming with technical diver's jargon. So, nothing here about respiratory minute volumes, surface air consumption rates or work of breathing measured in joules per litre. Also, I will make no reference to the fuzzy relationship to real values when gas pressure is used to measure gas volumes. (A practical but unscientific method full of wrong assumptions.) I also promise to not mention Moles, Avogadro's Postulate, or how important it is to know that different gases behave differently when under pressure. None of that, I promise.

What I will do instead is try to make the point using the simplest terms and examples possible. That point being that new technology, better equipment design and engineering, a broader understanding of teaching methods and what works, and a vastly bigger library of best practices, requires us to rethink old ideas.

Historically speaking, the Rule of Thirds has been the cave diving's default method of gas management since a guy named Sheck Exley dreamed it up in the 1970s. It has become an established convention that's based on how much gas a diver has in her or his cylinders at the beginning of the dive. The Rule of Thirds calls for the diver to use one third of that gas to swim into the overhead, one third for the swim back out to the cave entrance while keeping one third in reserve for emergencies.

So, it the simplest terms, if the pressure gauge attached to the cylinders showed 150 units of gas to start, the diver would breathe 50 going in, 50 coming out, and at the end of the dive would still have 50 units spare.

That spare gas is reserved for emergencies. And these fall into a bunch of categories. Perhaps the swim out takes longer or is harder work than the way in. Perhaps the diver gets tangled in something on her way out. Or perhaps a piece of kit breaks, and it takes time to sort things out to fix it well enough to call the dive and exit safely. Or perhaps a buddy (and divers are supposed to dive with at least one) has some sort of equipment failure and needs the gas carried by the first diver to swim out.

These emergencies bring up a full spectrum of problems... every colour, every wavelength: some potential and predominately hypothetical, several actual; all worth considering when planning to dive in an overhead environment.

In an earlier chapter, I wrote that I'd oversimplified the way this gas rule works and its effectiveness, so let's deal with things in more detail for the record, and to point out a major flaw.

Two divers (A and B) who are perfectly matched. They have similar levels of fitness, they consume diving gas at the same rate, they swim at the same pace, have matching experience and comfort levels. Also, their SCUBA cylinders are the same size, and set up with comparable bits and pieces, and contain exactly the same volume of diving gas. (In case you're detail oriented, let's pretend that gas analysed as a 32 percent nitrox, which at the maximum depth during their planned dive, is going to deliver an oxygen partial pressure of 1.184 bar.)

These two imaginary divers are simple traditionalists who follow Exley's suggested Rule of Thirds to the letter: one-third, two-thirds, home-free.

But let's imagine that while following the simplest possible scenario, their dive turns into an absolute mess. At the point of maximum penetration into the cave, where diver A and diver B have each used one-third of their gas and have signalled, 'let's turn our dive and head home', diver B has a sudden and total gas failure.

The probability of this happening is very, very unlikely. The probability of it happening when the divers are as far into the cave as they can go, is even more unlikely. However, we are considering the worst day possible, so that's what we are imagine happened.

When we plan for disaster, we plan around what's called the pinnacle dive. That means maximum depth, maximum time, and in this case, maximum penetration.

So, the worst-case scenario is, all the gas in diver B's cylinders is gone. Disappeared. Lucifer has poked his nose into things and so now both divers must share gas to swim to the exit.

When I wrote a few paragraphs back, "...their SCUBA cylinders are the same size, and set up with comparable bits and pieces...", in practical terms that means there is a second hose and regulator on each set of cylinders allowing two divers to breathe off the same cylinder set-up. They can therefore share gas and swim.

This takes a little practice, but that's all part of the process of learning to be a cave diver. However, in reality, it does slow down the journey from where the total gas failure happened, to the exit and fresh air. With two well-seasoned divers who've regularly practiced this sort of thing, a decent estimate is that their efficiency drops roughly ten percent. So, simple math, if they covered X metres on the way into the cave breathing from their own cylinders, they would need about 10 percent more time and gas to cover the same distance on the way out. That translates into a rather sad result. Diver A and Diver B run out of something to breath 90 percent of the way to fresh air and safety.

This of course is the best they could hope for, but it actually gets worse.

First problem is that it would be a remarkable diver who, faced with the total loss of their gas at the furthest penetration into a cave, could maintain the same calm breathing rate they enjoyed on the way in. Following the most basic consideration for variables in human nature, one could expect a few minutes at least of heightened angst; and that translates into heavier breathing, and that means using even more gas.

The second issue is another 'budget verses actual' situation. To make this scenario as simple as possible, I listed a bunch of assumptions early in the example scenario. The divers are using the same sized cylinders, filled to exactly the same pressure, have the same fitness level (which assumes similar stamina and ability to perform under pressure), and consume gas at the same rate. There's little chance that, in the real world, all these values would be the same, or even similar.

There are complex calculations and protocols to compensate for the vagaries of human physiology and the volume of gas different equipment carries. But these are not, by default, part of the basic calculations in the Rule of Thirds. And even when some additional allowances are made for different cylinders, different fill pressures, and different gas consumption rates at rest, there is not really anything to account for psychology and the way different people react to something going totally pear-shaped when fresh air is a 50-minute swim in one's future.

This, for me, is at the heart of the most important argument against relying on an out-dated rule to safeguard cave divers. At issue is the natural decay of all critical skills when they are not practiced and refreshed as part of a regularly scheduled update. The basic Rule of Thirds does not allow for this. It shouldn't be expected to since it's outside its purview. But it is a critical factor.

While most cave divers would agree that in a real gas-sharing emergency, it takes a while to calm down enough to gain control and synchronize actions with a buddy and to swim effectively while sharing gas. How long 'a while' is in minutes, and how much gas would be wasted, isn't well defined.

Nor is there a well-tested and proven factor to allow for the inefficiency of swimming while sharing gas. I mentioned a drop of ten percent efficiency earlier. This is a totally seat-of-the-pants guestimate, which warrants the usual <Your Milage May Vary> disclaimer.

This is so because swimming while sharing gas is NOT a skill certified cave divers practice often if at all. (While you'd be forgiven for thinking otherwise – given its potential to save one's backside – a straw poll conducted when researching this chapter indicated that fewer than one in five active cave divers had actually tried an air sharing drill over distance, inside a cave, since their initial training!)

Perhaps, I'm catastrophizing, but all in all, if things go completely pear-shaped at maximum penetration, it seems clear that many current suggestions get the team to a few hundred metres shy of the exit, before all hell breaks loose and everybody drowns.

And that was the premise of my magazine article, back in the dark ages when it was first published.

So, why is it that we don't swim past the remains of cave divers stacked like cordwood at the start of every dive?

Simply put, there are better options than the Rule of Thirds. In a worst-case scenario, every experienced cave diver has worked out (or been taught), it simply does not work, and to apply it as it stands is foolish.

The easiest fix is to cave dive in three-person buddy teams. For simplicity, again let's assume all three have the same size cylinders, carrying the same volume of gas, have very similar consumption rates and stress levels during their dive.

This new scenario is, we have divers A, B, and C, and one of them suffers a catastrophic gas failure. Now there are two lots of spare gas to get everyone home safely.

More common is to 'MODIFY' the Rule of Thirds. But these modified versions of the rule are far from standard. How much should it be modified? Should it be scrapped completely, or can its essence be salvaged? Is there a simple answer that works for most cases, or does it depend on who one asks?

A typical modification is to put an additional reserve aside, and what remains is divided into three portions, and the one third in, one third out, one third for emergencies rule is followed. The additional reserve is not factored into any of those calculations.

It's the size of the reserve that's at question.

When I taught, my suggestion was to use easy maths and, as a default, to use less than the usual 33 percent of the starting gas pressure to swim into the overhead. To make calculations easy to figure with <mental maths> we do this. Dealing with a fill of 210 bar, 55 bar is the magic number. The team swims into the cave until someone has used 55 bar of gas. So, the first team member whose pressure gauge reads 155 bar, signals their buddies and everyone turns the dive.

During the exit, a safe assumption is that all three will use approximately another 55 bar. They would reach the cave's exit, therefore, with approximately 100 bar left. Around half of their starting volume.

Of course, our divers could exit, but they would also have the luxury of taking their time on the way out and (after doing some recalculation), they can investigate things like side passages or simply dawdle, and really learn the cave and its secrets. There are plenty of 'it depends' provisos but instead of rushing out and learning nothing, they can put aside 85 bar for the exit. Using this method, they would arrive at the exit with approximately 70 bar remaining in their cylinders. That should sound familiar.

But doing this is not to everyone's taste. Mostly because it requires some thought, and is a different way to 'slice the cake', although perfectly within the normal safety margin.

More to the point, this method is not the Rule of Thirds, anymore, and for many would be *verboten*.

And then there is the problem of what to call it. Should it be called Overcoming Exley's Error, or Shuffling the Deck Differently or something else? It's certainly not following the status quo... and, in my opinion, nor should it.

It's time to update what we teach our student cave divers.

Question Fourteen

I WAS THINKING ABOUT GETTING INTO TECHNICAL DIVING… PERHAPS CAVE, BUT TRIMIX FOR SURE. WHAT'S STOPPING ME IS MY INSTRUCTOR WANTS ME TO SIGN A WAIVER AND GET MY HUSBAND'S SIGNATURE ON IT AS WELL. IS THIS NORMAL? IT DISTURBS ME, SO I REFUSED. WAS I RIGHT?

As an instructor and then as a member of an agency's training department, I'd get the occasional message like this, asking why we suggested every diver who'd decided to get involved in the so-called higher-risk activities – diving below recreational limits, or cave and wreck penetration diving – to provide proof they had explained to their significant other and their family that what they planned to do with us would subject them to increased risks. It seemed logical for us to ask them to let the folks close to them know, that from a training perspective, the goal posts had moved. But there was,

still is, always strong pushback. It's a question of shifted
responsibility.

Waivers and the constant threat of legal problems have driven the
dive industry into an awfully tight spot. And the blame for that is a
blameless society. The primary and secondary school systems in
England, Canada, and France have messed up. Those in particular,
since I have a passing familiarity with all three, and they perform less
and less well. It seems, the rot of 'zero responsibility' has set in and
become part of the ideas and beliefs of our time: society's zeitgeist.

I know several excellent young teachers who've dropped out
of those systems because they find it impossible to support, what
are now, "...the bent values that our classrooms and educational
systems represent".

More worrying are countries that ban books, challenge
science-based learning and refuse to teach topics as disturbing and
important as climate change. Or as interesting and innocuous as
evolution. These countries, the United States included, have a huge
and growing social impact. Critical thinking, and logic-based analysis
seem threatened, and common sense is taking a backseat to dogma
and superstition.

One hopes in all cases, especially the latter, that there are
more positive things going for the future of our species, than
education based on the banal, American Reality TV, the cartoon
characters who populate it, and paid meat promoting products on
social media that nobody needs. (And this from a marketing
executive!)

Perhaps our hope rests in the enlightened chance discoveries
awaiting the autodidactic child.

Just maybe, that's the fix: kids who push themselves to read grown-up and difficult books stuffed with real situations and adult responsibilities. However, my suggestion is, if that's the case, let's keep those young minds away, initially at least, from the novels of Miguel Asturias, Aleksandr Solzhenitsyn, and the complete works of Charles Dickens.

These three jokers totally corrupted and quashed my childhood glee, but don't misunderstand, this isn't a call to ban their books, just put them on a high shelf, out of reach of the young. And by doing so, let's give the smart kids a small reflection of hope as they deal with a clouded view through western society's crap-smeared windowpane as they grow!

And by the time this generation grows to make laws and map out what's taught in schools, let's hope those windows will have been cleaned, and the view will make more sense.

But this is about the relationship between a student wanting to sign up for an advanced diving program – cave diving – and the person teaching it.

Perhaps the biggest disappointment from a training point of view, is that as a group, through changing social mores, and diffident schooling, we have allowed ourselves to fall into the trap of waiting for someone else to fix things rather than fixing it for ourselves.

Apparently, most religious groups are waiting for the arrival of a messiah of one type or another. A saviour allows for something close to a universal shift of responsibility. A 'Jesus, take the wheel' – send more money, the pastor needs a new Lear Jet – kind of approach.

Even those calling themselves Jedis are waiting for a miracle to appear but like so many others, aren't doing much to make it happen themselves. Not visibly at least. Perhaps the Force, like the holy spirit and the comic-book Valkyrie, work in mysterious ways. Promoting progress and innovation is never easy. Enlightenment takes work. It's close and personal, and not a third-party, hands-off, waiting for the rapture, affair.

The point is that the responsibility – or more precisely having the integrity to take responsibility for one's actions and behaviour – isn't something one should shove onto someone else's lap. Jean-Paul Sartre, said a lot of things that go well above my head but one truth he's credited with is this: "[Humanity] is condemned to be free; because once thrown into the world, we are responsible for everything we do." That seems like pretty solid advice sent from an abundantly well-reasoned position, especially for a cave diver.

Now about this waiver. Specifically, not being willing to sign it. That is a showstopper, surprisingly common, and always begs the question, why on earth not? What is it they think they are giving up?

Part of being involved with a high-risk activity, from a zipline at the funfair, a camel ride around the Pyramid of Giza, or renting a jet ski to go tearing across a freshwater lake in Ontario, requires the people taking part to sign a waiver of some sort. Waivers are part of doing anything adventurous these days. All SCUBA diving courses from every major agency require one to be completed and signed. No exclusions.

The wording varies, but essentially, it's all about the person signing up for the experience, acknowledging that they understand there's risk involved in what they're about to do. They understand that, and they're willingly to accept responsibility and undertake the risk freely... as a grown-up, just as Sartre suggests. There's usually a clause that says the person taking the ride, taking part in the activity, or being a participant will not hold the person providing the experience liable if they get injured or experience some form of loss. It is a waiver of rights and liability, pure and simple.

There are complications, as there always are. Some regions of the world don't accept waivers as legal documents at all, and even in places where they do, a claim against a waiver is possible even when someone falls off the mechanical bull following a shower of Corona and six shots of agave tequila. That waiver is going to be disputed no matter how well- written, and even if signed by King Charles III and witnessed by the Archbishop of Canterbury.

Welcome to the 21st century.

So, if they are not totally valid and water-tight, why bother with waivers at all? And why ask for the student's partner or another close family member to co-sign?

Getting a signed waiver is about process and following the procedures a certifying dive agency requires its instructors to follow. Whether or not the document will stand up in court is, in every case, secondary.

However, asking for a waiver to be co-signed is unusual. It has nothing to do with process, and nothing much to do with lawyers and giving them purpose and a piece of paper to kick around and debate in a courtroom or in discovery – as entertaining as that might be. A waiver is an exercise in awareness, understanding, and to build a sort of trust between the student and instructor.

I don't have stats for the number of prospective students an active (and conscientious) instructor or instructor trainer turns away in her career. But it happens. More often at the higher levels of instruction such as for a cave diving class.

Sometimes the instructor gets a sense that their potential student has issues following instructions and will question and resist any suggestions for change and growth or compliance. Let's call it a sixth-sense alarm: a Spiderman sense. Often, these students pay their money and believe that entitles them to a pass. But of course, no dive class at any level works that way... and certainly not a cave class.

These are the potential customers who are refunded their money and waved off early in the instructor/student relationship; often before anyone gets close to the classroom, workshop, or water. Refusing to sign a waiver, and not understanding what's at play when asked to get a life-partner to co-sign is a huge 'tell'. It indicates deep-seated issues.

In a litigious society, these are the customers who'll sue because the water was too cold, or the coffee was too hot, or the cave furniture is too pointy, or the course too hard.

Asking a candidate for a cave class to sign and share a waiver, therefore, is a sort of litmus test. Are they up for the challenge and are they comfortable with everything the challenge brings? Are they a grown-up? Do they understand their role in this learning gig? I'm sure there are better metrics, but this all we have.

A beginner's dive class – an open water class – the instructor is surrounded by novices who need – and understandably expect – their hands to be held from beginning to end. If there were a big gauge showing who's responsible for what, with the student at one end and the instructor at the other, the needle would be a mouse's-nose-width away from suggesting the instructor's responsibility is close to 100 percent.

As the complexity and difficulty of the program being taught increases, that needle swings relentlessly further from the instructor alone and approaches the middle, and by the time it comes to cave diving, the burden is shared evenly. By the time a class of cave students (a maximum of three, by the way), the instructor is essentially diving with peers. Not quite peers perhaps, but individuals who – as team members – willingly carry their share of the burden of care.

So, understand what that waiver is about and sign it!

Question Fifteen

I HEARD YOU TALK AT A DIVE SHOW AND YOU MENTIONED CARRYING A STAGE BOTTLE ON CAVE DIVES. WILL YOU EXPLAIN WHY AND HOW THAT WORKS?

Although I've tried to stay general and non-technical with the answers herein – since it isn't intended as a how-to book, and I wanted to keep things relevant for a wider audience – I've included this for a couple of reasons. First, it might help folks who are not cave divers get a better idea of the kind of details that overhead divers include in their dive planning... something a long, long way removed from seat-of-the-pants guesswork. Secondly, it might offer helpful tips to a cave diver or someone starting out as a cave diver. And finally, it might also be a useful primer for any diver interested in some elementary gas planning advice. So here it is.

Stage bottle... that's an interesting term, isn't it? To a non-diver there's little in the way of clues in the name. To a certified diver, depending on where they learned to dive and with whom, any clues they do find might just as readily lead to a dead end as to an answer. So, let's define what's meant in this case, and since my technique is pretty much standard, how I use it.

A stage bottle is an extra cylinder filled with the same gas carried in the primary cylinders. Diving most of my favourite caves in Mexico, all three of the cylinders I carry – the two primaries and the stage – are filled with a bog-standard nitrox with roughly 32 percent oxygen in it. This gives me slightly longer time in the water without needing to decompress, compared with doing the same dive while breathing air. Actually, all that's a little academic since most of the fill stations in Mexico's cave country don't bother pumping air at all. Nitrox is what they normally put in cylinders and stages. Anything else would be a special request.

The stage is also fitted with a regulator and pressure gauge, and it's rigged so it can be carried at my side: my left side. It fits neatly underneath the primary cylinder that also hangs on that side. (I prefer a sidemount configuration which basically means that the two primary cylinders are attached to my sides, parallel to my body's lateral line). On a good day, all these cylinders behave and stay where they're put; streamlined, out of the way, and relatively non-intrusive.

WHY BOTHER WITH A THIRD CYLINDER?

The, 'why bother to do it?' question is easy to answer. The extra gas in the stage bottle allows me to extend my in-water time and travel a little further into the cave. And that's the main point of carrying a third cylinder: to travel further. In addition, the method I use adds a degree of safety that most divers find comforting. I certainly find it so.

I'll try to explain details about the gas management of carrying a third cylinder, and why doing so adds a margin of safety in a while. Let's get some more naming conventions out of the way first.

On occasion, a third cylinder, the same size and shape as a stage bottle, filled with exactly the same gas as a stage bottle, rigged and carried the same as a stage bottle, isn't a stage bottle. It's a buddy bottle. The difference is that it's used as stand-by in the event of something going particularly pear-shaped. The gas in it is only used to supply gas that would normally be donated by a buddy in an emergency. That's the only time it's deployed. So, although it is carried throughout a dive, it would be as full at the end of the dive as it was the beginning. Untouched. Unless something nasty and unexpected happened.

I've often carried a buddy bottle when taking less experienced divers into a cave they're unfamiliar with, as a 'belt and suspenders' manoeuvre to help them feel more comfortable, and to provide me with a sense of well-being. To date, I have used a buddy bottle only once, and even then, it didn't play a truly critical role. That said, I still carry one when circumstances dictate. It's a little like carry a spare red plastic container of gasoline on a long car journey. If I have it, chances are excellent that it's not going to be needed. Obviously better that than the other way around.

Extra cylinders can also be used to carry gas to optimize decompression in the final stages of a dive that's been particularly long or deep or both. These 'decompression cylinders' carry a gas containing more oxygen, and therefore a lower percentage of the inert gas than in the primaries, or stage bottle, or buddy bottles. Two classic blends are a deco gas containing 50 percent oxygen (which can be used from around 21 metres and shallower), and one with 100 percent oxygen for use at six metres and above.

There are conventions covering gas management for all these different types of cylinders but let me explain the method I use and recommend for cave diving with stage bottles.

USING STAGE BOTTLES

The traditional gas management method for use with a stage, is to treat the gas it carries the same as the primary gas supply: breathe one-third on the way in, one-third on the way out, and leave one-third for contingencies. If nothing hits the fan on a dive following this method, divers surface with stages and primary cylinders about one-third full.

While following this method isn't wrong, I believe there's a way to manage things that's more right.

This better option is called "half + 15." This method requires a little more thought and slightly more careful arithmetic, but it's considered more conservative than the traditional method and, because of that, better.

Again, if everything goes smoothly using this method, divers surface with stages close to empty, but with all the contingency gas in their primary cylinders, which – with a single stage – translates into the primaries (twins or sidemount) being around half-full or more at the end of the dive. (Read on to find out how this works!)

Having all this gas left over may seem wasteful to a non-diver, or a recreational diver used to arrive back on the dive boat after a bimble on a reef or open wreck, with nothing but seeds and stems. However, a reminder that – for a cave diver – the option of swimming directly to the surface (which is simply 'up' for a recreational diver) doesn't exist.

First, I have to explain some logistics and define a couple of variables, so that the following example is as simple and as brief as I can manage.

In Mexico, the default cylinders are bog-standard 11 litre aluminum. If you have walked into a dive shop almost anywhere in the world and seen SCUBA tanks, chances are good they were these. Eleven litre aluminum SCUBA tanks have an interior volume of 11 litres. If we filled one with German lager, drinking water, cow's milk, M&Ms, or gin, it would hold 11 litres of the stuff. Predictably, if we poured out the beer, water, milk, sweeties, and gin, an 11-litre cylinder also holds 11 litres of air. This should make sense to you.

A quick note. In the non-metric world (the USA), these cylinders are known as 80s because they are supposed to hold 80 cubic feet of gas when filled to the suggested working pressure of 3,000 pounds per square inch (AKA psi). If you find that slightly baffling, it gets worse. An aluminum 80 SCUBA tank does NOT hold that volume of gas at 3,000 psi. It holds less. This and other nonsense are among the reasons why the rest of the world is metric.

PUMP IT UP!

Anyway, back to our nice logical metric 11-litre cylinder. We need to fill it with something to breathe, and that requires it to be connected to a compressor. A compressor pumping SCUBA – quality gas is very different to the air compressor at your local garage or paintball station. To begin with, it's fitted with a complex filtration system that removes impurities and anything that's not gas, including water vapour. (Typically, compressed air for diving has a dew point in the minus 40 range. It's dry!)

Scuba compressors can also compress gas to extremely high pressures. When an 11-litre cylinder is full, the gas inside is at 210 times normal atmospheric pressure. Put another way, rather than it containing only 11 litres of air, there are 210 times 11 litres in there when it's full. Quick multiplication, that's a total of 2,310 litres.

That would be a lot of M&Ms and I don't know how many litres of gin the average adult consumes in a minute, but the average calm and experienced diver breathes around 12-14 litres of gas per minute on the surface. (That's around one tankful of gas normal atmospheric pressure, and a full tank contains 210 times that.)

Quick division: that one tank of compressed gas would last the average diver 210 minutes. That's three and a half hours if they sat in a deck chair on the lawn, watching squirrels chasing each other around a maple tree. When diving, it wouldn't last that long.

First of all, diving is more strenuous than sitting on a deck chair, and also the pressure underwater increases as one goes deeper. As an example, in a cave in Mexico, at a total depth of say 20 metres, the ambient pressure would be three times what it is on the surface. And to breathe – disregarding all the other factors such as task loading and swimming effort – a diver would use a little more than three times the density or volume of gas they'd use on the surface. So instead of 12 litres each minute, they'd use 36, and the gas in that 11-litre tank would last only one hour instead of three and a half.

Hopefully, all this makes some sense. However, as nice as it is to have some background info., it doesn't explain stage tanks and how to use them.

The normal procedure is to start one's dive breathing from the stage. This is the same regardless of which gas management method is being followed. When the pre-arranged volume of gas in the stage has been used (according to either method), the diver switches to breathing from their primary gas supply. At this point, the stage could be dropped someplace ready to be picked up on the way back out. The swim into the cave continues until the turn-around point is reached. On the way out, the stage bottle is picked up and the diver switches to breathing from it until the exit.

That's the Coles Notes[9] version.

WARNING HALF+15 EXPLAINED... NUMBERS FOLLOW!

The 'Half+15' method I use with a stage refers to just that. I want there to be half of the starting pressure plus 15 bar to be in my stage when I make the switch to breathing from my primary cylinders. In other words, I can use a little less than half of the volume of the stage bottle (15 bar less) before shutting it down and switching. But what's a 'bar'?

---

[9] Coles Notes are student guides to literature and how-to books published in Canada. The value of them was that the student did not have to read the whole book to write a book review for their class. Therefore, Coles Notes are a shortcut.

Back to the power of using metric (SI units). One bar is the pressure of one atmosphere. That's the pressure around you now as you read this page. (Unless you're reading this while sitting in a space craft or at the bottom of the ocean in an underwater habitat, or halfway up Mount Kilimanjaro.) You may recall, a few paragraphs back, I mentioned that when full, SCUBA tanks contain gas at around 210 times normal atmospheric pressure: another way to put that is 210 bar. And that's how divers speak.

There is a little pressure gauge attached to the stage bottle (well, there would be one attached to all three bottles, the primaries, and the stage). Pressure gauges are graduated in bar, and at the beginning of my dive, it would have read 210.

So, when it's time to switch to breathing from my primaries, it'll read 120 bar indicating that there was a half plus 15 bar left. My safe margin! (Another way to interpret this is that I have consumed around 90 bar: a half MINUS 15. If you are scratching your head and saying to yourself, 'hold on, that means there are 30 bar difference there in favour of the gas remaining in the stage bottle', welcome to the world of contingency, cover your backside, gas planning.)

As an aside, one of the advantages of using the same sized cylinders for primaries and the stage, is that the arithmetic is easier. It's done once. All the values are similar and easy to remember. More so when they are written down. So, once calculations are done, they don't have to do them again!

One more note. The standard starting pressure in aluminum cylinders is at around 210 bar. Any over-fill (a pressure above 210 bar) is a bigger safety cushion. A prudent diver still uses only 90 bar from the stage. This keeps an even larger volume of contingency gas safe in the stage.

At the beginning of this, I mentioned that using this method rather than thirds, all contingency gas is carried in the primary cylinders. If you were paying attention, you may have been wondering how come this method allows the diver to use ALL the gas in the stage bottle? This is why.

Let me explain how that works. A sidemount diver has two primary cylinders and, for this exercise, they are considered independent systems; both available to the diver, but each with a regulator, a pressure gauge and probably another hose for inflating things like a drysuit or a buoyancy cell.

The "third" reserve in a stage bottle would amount to 70 bar of breathing gas (one third of 210 bar). So, to keep that safe and available for emergencies, we account for it by splitting that gas between the two primary cylinders: 35 bar in each.

Here's the magic. We simply take 35 bar from the 210 bar in each primary. That leaves 175 bar. This is the value of the gas we can use now. We calculate thirds using this value. One third of 175 is 58 and a bit. Let's err on the side of safety and call 58 and a bit, 55. Therefore, when we have used 55 bar from each primary we turn the dive and head home.

A quick recap: I start the dive breathing from my stage bottle. When the pressure gauge shows 120 bar left, I shut the valve on that bottle and begin breathing from my main cylinders. When the pressure gauges on each of those cylinders shows 155 bar of gas left, I call the dive and head home. All things being equal, when the "second third" in my primaries has been used, and the pressure gauges on each of them shows around 100 bar, I should have arrived back at my stage bottle (which convention suggests I leave somewhere safe on the way in), pick it up, check it, turn it on and breathe from it all the way back to the surface and fresh air.

And at the end of the dive, the stage will be close to empty, and all the contingency gas for this dive will be in my primaries which will show a pressure of around 100 bar... close to half of what I started with.

To justify the advantages of doing this – over leaving contingency gas in the stage – requires a white board and plugging through various disaster scenarios. All that belongs in a cave stage diver class (or a RAID Cave 2 manual), and not in a chapter in a non-how-to book.

Yes, using Half+15 does require using a piece of paper and checking your numbers a few times, but we just did that! You're good to go! (...I guess this IS a how-to book after all.)

Question Sixteen

*I TOOK A RESCUE CLASS WITH **** THROUGH MY LOCAL DIVE SHOP AND IT WAS A REAL BUMMER. I LEARNED NOTHING USEFUL. IS THERE ANOTHER COURSE YOU'D RECOMMEND THAT WILL TEACH ME SKILLS THAT WILL HELP IN AN EMERGENCY?*

Most SCUBA rescue classes fall short of being truly helpful. We could throw SCUBA First-Aid programs into the wastebin too. I cannot single out one agency: most fall short. It's both lame and disingenuous to think that in one two-day weekend and a couple of dives, a punter leaves the average rescue class with any skill besides remembering to make sure to keep an unconscious diver's airway open when swimming them to the surface.

There used to be a pub in Northwest London called The Rossetti. Due to the unfortunate march of urban renewal, it's gone now, closed to make way for a block of flats.

If you're an art snob, a Beatles Fan (Abbey Road Studios is close by), or you have an address in NW8, you may remember it. The pub, named after Dante Gabriel Rossetti (surprisingly a British pre-Raphaelite painter) sold decent beer and excellent sandwiches. Unusual for its time in the history of English kitchen arts, they contained more filling than bread. Its heyday was also around the birth of the real ale movement, and the beer was from a local brewery, and it was excellent too. In short, Rossetti's was a great place to enjoy an after-work pint and a light supper.

It was an 'up-market' place with its walls hung with reproductions of mid-19th century paintings from the Pre-Raphaelite Brotherhood. Works by Hunt, Millais, Burne-Jones, Morris; and pride of place went to huge copy of Rossetti's Proserpine, hanging behind the bar next to an ornate faux Art Nouveau mirror. It was all quite spectacular and special: a restful place, and quite smart for the ruffians in my peer group.

On my last visit, a friend from out of town – an art director with an eye for these things – pointed out to the owner that one of the paintings was definitely out of place and needed to be taken down.

The Three Fates, by Alexander Rothaug looks pre-Raphaelite but isn't. The owner of the pub, a big man, a surly curmudgeon who looked capable of lifting all three Fates and their apparatus with one hand, asked if my friend had attended art school. She admitted she had and named a private college in Los Angeles. The owner swore – only half under his breath – and calling her a "typical interfering American twat", asked what bloody difference it made to anything at all, and walked off.

My friend called after him, "That painting is an imposter! It's here under false pretenses! It's wrong! If you had any comprehension of art, you'd take it down right now." And just like that, we were banned, never to darken the doors of The Rossetti again.

FIND THE IMPOSTERS... THEY'RE EVERYWHERE!

Weeding out the imposters, always creates a disturbance. You may be correct to do so, but there is usually a price to pay.

SCUBA diving is far different from most other outdoor adventures. It's not like back-country hiking, wilderness camping, technical mountain biking, white-water rafting, or a bunch of related activities.

After things go absolutely pear-shaped when someone has walked off-grid and falls off the edge of the map or gets caught in an unseasonal snowstorm on the side of a mountain, they have time available to process the situation and come up with a solution.

Broken gear, broken bones, getting lost, and a dramatic change in the weather, all allow hours or even days for the unfortunate punter to work things out. However, in most survival emergencies under the waves, SCUBA divers have seconds or minutes to react.

There are other imperatives too; some related to time, some not so much so. One is training and how it's processed and promoted; and perhaps most of all, how it's labelled. Few divers truly understand they're being sold a fake; an imposter posing as something useful that isn't.

There was a full-page ad in one of the online mags that landed in my inbox a while ago. It was for a wilderness survival school. It was a fine-looking ad. Lots of lean, clean youthful folks dressed in North Face and Columbia fabrics portaging carbon-fibre canoes and carrying state-of-the-art backpacks.

Not a scratch, chipped gunnel, unzipped pocket, mud stain or greasespot anywhere to be seen. And no sweaty, dirty faces looking out from the page.

The ad was selling three- and five-day training courses at something called a survival school. Although the images used were suspiciously art-directed and looked nothing like any outdoor trip I've been part of, they did manage to get the point across. Survival School seemed like an extremely good idea.

According to the ad copy, participants would learn the basic skills needed to get by in Canada's wilderness if something hit the fan while on the trail.

The list included how to build shelter, forage for food, light a fire, tend to injuries, signal for help; all were included in the three and five-day package. It got me thinking about divers and what training we have in the world of SCUBA to build similar, but more appropriate skills; to survive diving mishaps.

Looking at SCUBA and freediving courses, taking them apart and thinking about how each of them fits the needs of divers, is part of the job for folks who work in a dive agency, therefore part of my shtick. The opinions formed during this process are what generates the push for new programs and what points out the need to update existing ones.

Considering all those issues, there might be a hole. I can't decide whether it's in the curriculum or the way we push the concept of survival, but there's a gap in there somewhere.

You don't have to be a professor of semantics to know, words are powerful. Survival is an example of that. It's a strong word with powerful associated mental images. Also, and maybe because of the images it conjures, it's not part of the language we use to market diving.

The questions are: Should it be, and if it were, what would have to change? How differently would we teach or talk to students? More to the point, would a class in survival techniques be popular with divers? Is it necessary given what's currently taught? What would it teach — since how to light a fire in a snowstorm at 3,000 meters on the side of a mountain with nothing but a candy bar, a handful of cotton wool, and a ski pole — isn't going to prepare a diver for the unexpected?

One can argue that a soft-edged form of survival school does exist in diving. If you have ever taken a technical diving class, you have most likely sat through an accident analysis module. It's an important part of those classes. Otto von Bismarck, said a fool learns from his own experience, but it's better to learn from the experience of others. That's the thinking behind including accident analysis as part of a tech-diving course.

The shame is that the concept doesn't extend to every level of diver training. Perhaps you've heard an instructor or dive shop owner laugh and say, "We don't want to frighten customers away, do we?", when the topics of accident analysis and risk management are mentioned.

I don't have an answer to that. Ron Watters does.

Watters, Professor Emeritus of Outdoor Education at Idaho State University, when researching serious accidents in white-water paddling wrote: "The question is: how can we as outdoor educators prepare ourselves and our staff to make the 'right' decision when faced with a potentially dangerous situation? Experience is always the best teacher, but short of being involved or being on-hand during actual river accidents, the next best way of preparing ourselves is through the study of river accidents."

That's another vote in favour of accident analysis, but is that one module in a technical diving program enough?

The Academy of Management Journal uses the term "vicarious learning," to describe the process of "acquiring the complex sequence of behaviour without having to execute the behaviour."

I wonder if that would be more palatable to the several diving agencies who've opted to sell SCUBA diving as a 'low-risk activity'.

Would renaming an accident analysis module 'Vicarious Learning' mean diving instructors would be cleared to tell students that diving can be dangerous and ignoring rules and breaking standards could get them hurt. Would the infidelity of the 'low risk' label be explained honestly before open water students hand over their credit card and sign a waiver?

That's a lot of questions, and maybe they are a result of overthinking the situation and overreacting to the growing number of diving-related fatalities. But questions seem justified, given the numbers.

The estimated hospital emergency room admissions in the USA for the five years ending in 2020, indicated that bowling injuries logged more than 15,000 visits while SCUBA diving rolled in with just a handful more than 1,500. Statistically then, we could say something like 'Scuba diving is only a tenth as risky as tenpin bowling'. Armed with that data, there is the potential for some dubious headlines. Several dive agency marketing departments have jumped at the opportunity. And in case you think that's just a cynical opinion, and that kind of nonsense wouldn't make it out of the first creative meeting, it truly already has.

Missing from those numbers, of course, is the relative severity of the related injuries. A dislocated finger stuck in a bowling ball, compared to problems from pathological air trapping, or breath holding while ascending from a dive, for instance. So, once again, any comparison between bowling and SCUBA diving would never be used by a responsible company, would it? Nobody would have the stones to try to float that misdirection in its marketing, surely?

If diving were in fact safer than bowling, nothing would need to change. But it is not. As I write this, four divers have died in the space of a couple of weeks, in North America alone. No reports of four dead in a bowling alley in North America or any place else.

In his book, *Deep Survival*, Laurance Gonzales tells his readers only 10-20 percent of people can stay calm in the midst of a survival emergency. For everyone in that sort of situation, survival is a roll of the dice, but the odds in favour of a positive outcome, improve for those who can keep their cool.

I'm unaware of similar stats for divers. My guess is that it's a similar story. For the eight out of ten who don't stay calm when faced with a situation that threatens their life, many muddle through somehow with nothing more than phycological scars. Injury enough, one suspects. Sadly, occasionally, some don't make it at all.

Gonzales – and others who look analytically at risk, survival, and people's reactions when faced with a nasty surprise – write about hot and cold cognition. Hot being when emotion drives our reaction to an event, compared to cold which is when we stop, observe, think, and act. Put another way, cold cognition is an executive brain function vs the freeze, fight, or flight signals we get from our limbic cortex as a result of hot cognition.

Specialized instruction may be an answer. At the very least, I believe, it would be an honest answer. And that might be a good start for the SCUBA industry to consider.

Let's look again at what the dive industry offers in the way of training. Specifically, training that includes survival skills.

In open water training, we could start off by making as sure as possible, that everyone about to take part is fit. They would not have to be an athlete, but a moderate level of aerobic capacity and able to do a few push-ups... and certainly they should have the ability to swim. Some agencies do not require this.

Students are also instructed to dive with a buddy. In more advanced programs (cave diving for instance), it's suggested that having two buddies, and diving as part of a team of three, is even better. See above.

As a beginner, it's also explained that diving in an overhead environment – a cavern, a cave, a wreck, or any kind of swim-through – requires special equipment, training, and experience, well beyond open water, or even open water instructor. The stats and basic common-sense shout loudly that following this advice is a great survival tactic.

Another bulkhead against surprises is to inspect gear and do a buddy check before starting a dive. Every dive. At the open water level these checks are basic but need to be stressed. Various mnemonics and prompts are offered up to help the process along. In addition, many instructors have added to the basic training they deliver, the technical diver's habit of using a physical checklist.

One final topic that should be covered from day one, is the solid advice to test and get used to operating new gear, one piece at a time, in a 'controlled environment'. For those of us without access to a sheltered, shallow cove, with stellar visibility and zero water movement, this means a swimming pool.

Noting, all these would make for a brilliant start.

Most dive agencies offer advanced courses referred to as 'Rescue Diver', or the like. The desired outcome of these is to produce a diver capable of helping another diver to survive.

These courses often teach great additional SCUBA skills, but they are not survival skills. Roughly half the in-water time is spent on diver recovery rather than rescue, and most of the remainder on performing 'rescue breaths' on the surface. This seems skewed in the wrong direction. These are not survival skills. They are recovery and surface rescue skills.

But unfortunately, this type of program is firmly accepted, is popular, and only partly appropriate in so far as it reinforce the basics taught in the open water program. Repetition, reminders, practice, all perfectly bona fide. All with immense potential value. But not survival.

The few courses that teach independent diving, also called 'solo diving', come closer. But these have an attached stigma, given that diving is marketed as a team activity. Therefore, these courses send a mixed message. Solo diving has a rotten aura to it. But the idea that a diver can, when things fall off the rails, help herself and her teammates to survive by making the correct decisions, is golden.

Because of this, we might best interpret this course as something other than 'solo'. Perhaps this course is the closest we come to actual survival training, and delivery of basic accident theory and awareness in regular diver instruction.

So, if the dive industry has all this going for it, why change things; why add another course?

The simple answer is that what's in place is being ignored. And if not ignored, then fudged; seriously fudged.

A very superficial analysis of the four recent deaths mentioned earlier seems to prove this. Sadly, two divers died in an overhead, when neither had training to be in that environment. One other seems to have had a serious health issue, while attempting a dive in challenging conditions. The fourth started his dive disconnected from the rest of his team and died alone.

Without much effort and little prior knowledge — other than how to do a google search — anyone of us could pull up handfuls of miserable examples all following pathways to the same or similar outcomes.

Goethe writes that we learn by seeking and blundering we learn. However, Goethe was a writer and not a diver. Blundering along while breaking the basic rules, is not the best, certainly not the safest way to learn about diving, and it is not a part of a valid survival mindset.

It will always be impossible to stop all blundering, but we can, at the very least, hope to lessen its prevalence and impact. Death by errors of omission, commission, misadventure or oversight, are a wholly unacceptable outcome to someone going for a recreational dive.

Explorers may have an excuse to push the limits, and function on the other side of best practice. Their excuses may be weak and filled with hubris and ego, but they are explorers, and as such, have prepared themselves to face a crushing outcome. They have, by the very nature of what they do, made a statement of intent. Not an intent to die, but a clear agreement that they understand and have accepted the odds. They are willingly throwing dice and gambling fate.

However, the person who drives a cement truck, or arranges flowers, or works in an hospital, a coffee shop or bakery does none of that. They went for a bimble and died.

How far removed from what they projected as a future outcome that reality must be.

So where does that leave us? Another question.

The best answer I have is, more training. There is an irony or contradiction of terms or some flaw of logic in that argument but it's the best I can do.

Perhaps there's room for a restructured program or maybe a three- or five-day workshop format built around the concept of survival, independence, and awareness. A course that admits Gonzales' suggestion that fear puts you in your place and gives you the humility you need to see things in perspective.

That may be a workable solution. A real survival school for divers. Socrates said I cannot teach anybody anything, I can just make them think. If that's true, the dive industry should look for a stronger catalyst, because it really needs to get more people to think and demand better results from the courses being offered. Because as it stands to date, the SCUBA survival training on offer is as bogus as an Alexander Rothaug painting being labelled as pre-Raphaelite.

Question Seventeen

DO YOU USE A CHECKLIST FOR CAVE DIVING AND WHAT MNEMONIC DO YOU PREFER TO MAKE SURE YOU STAY ON TRACK?

Pre-dive checklists are a brilliant idea. While it'd be a dreadful misdirection to suggest using one is a panacea for all that's wrong in the world, when designed well and used correctly prior to a complicated task, like cave diving, a checklist can be a true boon. In the past five years or so, there has been a real push from the CCR (rebreather) diving community to make checklists part of the prep for every dive, and that idea is spilling over onto the "getting-ready" stage of open-circuit dives... but I have to put in a plug for cave divers, who've been using their version for decades: and it isn't a mnemonic or a piece of laminated cardboard.

I'm not a fan of the classic memory-jogging prompts that SCUBA agencies teach open water divers to run through at the start of a dive. These usually take the form of a bunch of initials forming a questionable and unclear acronym, which is usually condensed-speak for a series of checks that divers should run tick off before getting their ears wet.

Traditionally these are something like: G.R.A.F.T.E.R. or B.E.W.A.R.R.E or B.A.R.A.F.T.A or something equally optimistic and silly, where each initial represents something that needs to be checked and confirmed. The usual suspects are Buoyancy, Weights, Releases, Air-pressure, Buddy gear check, Confirmation of dive plan, and Go! I've probably missed a bunch of things, because, as mentioned, mnemonics simply do not work for me.

As far as they go, these verbal gymnastics are a paper-thin improvement over screaming "Tally-Ho chaps," like an Eton old boy and launching oneself into the ocean cannonball style. But if we're serious about a full checklist, there's a lot to add to the average implausible open water diver checklist.

Personally, as well as those things, I'd like to confirm with my buddy what gas I'm breathing (since one-third of it or more is for them). Knowing the maximum depth I can breathe it at, and how much of it there is in my tanks, are good additions for the same reason. Checking that my regulators work (especially the one I'd donate in a gas-sharing emergency), how much gas I intent to leave for that potential gas-sharing episode: and so on, are all nice things to share too.

And what about confirming what a few waypoints, like go-no-go times, turn-around times, depth and length of a safety stop for example before my buddy and I set out on our adventure? how long our dive is going to be; where we are hoping to go, and what we expect to see when we get there are fine things to check as well? The list is a long one and none of this is spurious or factitious. My guess is that recreational buddy teams get things like this confused on plenty of dives. They muddle through, but is muddling through and maybe missing the point of the dive what we should be aiming for?

The checklist habit for rebreather divers follows the examples used in aviation and medicine. Following that lead, an actual physical checklist is recommended. Something real that can be read from rather than pulled from memory. So, a piece of paper or an active screen that can be marked <DONE> with a marker or stylus. Something that can be used as part of an audit trail, or at least until the flight is over and the plane is back in the hanger, the patient is in recovery, or everyone is back on the surface with a smile on their face.

Most of us do this sort of thing for a grocery list, why not do it to help get the most out of a dive?

However, suggesting any of this to the average diver, even a technical diver, and changes are you will draw blank stares or pitiful looks and shaken heads. Those folks are unlikely to bother with a fancy notebook strapped across their knee, a Chinagraph grease pencil in hand, working their way down a list of things to check. An enlightened few will, but a minority. There's solid resistance from CCR divers too despite most manufacturers supplying printable lists in their user manuals.

One noted CCR diver's excuse for not using a physical checklist goes something like: 'if you need a list, you have no business diving the unit...' implying that everyone owning a rebreather is blessed with an eidetic memory. Not many do, and a rebreather, although a simple concept, can have dozens of seemingly trivial things, costing as little as a few cents, that can turn a $15,000 expedition grade CCR into a fancy paperweight. A physical checklist for assembly and predive helps prevent that sort of thing happening. It's not foolproof, but is better than relying on, what as we age, becomes an increasingly dodgy memory.

Perhaps the best midpoint, a meeting of the minds, and an acceptable compromise is the checklist concept used by cave divers. Not everyone of them, but certainly ones who are cautious and avoid silly mistakes.

It's physical but not necessarily written, and is a simple call and response, just like a good blues song.

The dive leader will begin the process by starting at their head and working down to their feet explaining each piece of kit as they go. So, it might sound something like:

1) I'm wearing a 3mm hood and it's comfy

2) I have on my mask, it's defogged, I checked the strap and it's fine

3) I have two regulators around my neck, the primary will be in my mouth, it's on a standard long hose connected to the cylinder on my right side, and it is the one that's for you should you need gas. The other is hanging on a bungee necklace is connected to the cylinder on my left side. It's mine!

And so on. In between each step, the leader's buddy or buddies will take an opportunity to check their kit and once checked will respond with a 'yes,' 'check,' or an explanation what's different and why.

It sounds pedantic but gets quite detailed when the leader gets to their tanks and explains what gas is in them, the maximum safe operating depth of that gas, how many bar there are, what the turn-pressure will be, and so on. Same with it comes time to check the settings on their dive computer, or the contents of the pouch which many sidemount divers hang above their bum.

This is when the toolkit is discussed. Who has the very expensive marine-grade crescent wrench (adjustable spanner), who has cable-ties, how many spare masks are there, how many spare mouthpieces, orings, backup lights, nut drivers, double-ended bolt snaps, and how many metres of bungee and paracord are shared among the group?

And if this sounds over-the-top, it isn't. It's just part of that pre-dive checklist. Some, maybe most, recreational divers carry what's called a save-a-dive kit to the dive site. Cave divers bring there's on the dive. Because there's nothing fun having a broken light handle a 90-minute swim into the dark.

Being able to hand the poor soul at the end of this inconvenience a tool or a cable-tie guarantees you at least two free beers at the end of the dive. Amazingly, in the instant when the fan begins to spin and one hears the scraping sound of a shovel, being handed a solution in the form of a tool or a buddy's back up, or cable tie or a piece of bungie dissolves any fear, flattens rising discomfort and brightens black thoughts. Mentally ticking that particular box before at the start of a dive is golden.

And so, it turns out that when you're suited up and ready to dive open-circuit, chances are good you are wearing a workable checklist.

Question Eighteen

I REALLY ENJOYED THE COLUMNS YOU USED TO WRITE FOR TECHNICAL DIVER MAGAZINE. ARE THEY PUBLISHED IN A BOOK, SOMEWHERE?

I find getting the rare request like this one are a great ego boost. They almost inevitably arrive in the inbox on the black days when one wakes up asking "Why is there a cat sleeping on my head?" "Should I bother to get up today or just stay here and do nothing all day?" It's especially neat when you're getting credit for work that isn't yours. You see, I have never written a column or anything else for Techdiver Magazine. However, I do write columns and here are three of them from the distant past.

The internet changed the game entirely, but not altogether in quite the way we expected. Ben Elton tells us that it was supposed to 'liberate knowledge.' In its infancy, with pockets stuffed full of innocent intent and looking out at the world through rose-tinted spectacles, it did. Then the digital equivalent of Dutch Elm Disease set in. After the initial rush, knowledge became buried under what Elton writes is a 'vast sewer of ignorance, laziness, bigotry, superstition and filth and then beneath the cloak of political surveillance.'

And that's what happened to the game: a huge, baffling sea change that moved the sidelines and stands, and then installed locked gates across the goalmouths.

It was amusing at first. Amusing until the reality set in and then it was alarming to watch the online world's evolution and distressing slide towards the extinction of grace and humanity from the inside.

I ran an early online chat room, a sort of social network cum virtual community for divers. This was when less informed recreational dive agencies and the old-school instructors teaching for them, rallied against anything they didn't control or sell tickets to – staged decompression diving, breathing any gas other than compressed air, wearing more than one cylinder, diving deeper than 40 metres – they flipped out. Their outrage and indignation was epic.

So, for those of us doing and teaching those things – newly baptised as technical diving – the little chat room was a place of refuge, where the proverbial like-minded souls could exchange ideas and give advice when asked.

My memories may be more Polly Anna than they actually deserve, but it was where people could debate the value of ABC decompression gas versus something else, where one could find someone to share a deck plan of XYZ shipwreck, and where people were willing to teach and learn.

There were blowhards. The boastful, who wasted column-inches exaggerating what they'd done and how often. There were egoists trying to kill the vibe through their self-focussed sense of superiority and lack of empathy. But these were a tepid minority.

The rest were a trip to read postings from and share stories with. Most gave and tried hard to be helpful. It was a community of those willing to share, and more than a few, quietly accomplished things that set a precedent because they were an example of what a new approach to SCUBA diving could lead to.

But very soon, too soon, technical diving became a sport instead of a crazy diversion from corporate life, a distraction, and pure entertainment. Sport, yes, that's an unfortunate word and used intentionally. Sports have winners and losers. In fact, sport is about winning more than participating. Yes, sport is something technical diving should never have become. However, it did.

Perhaps it was only a few people who wanted control, but it seemed like overnight the postings turned from helpful and chummy to lies and half-truths. Instead of useful tips and suggestions on how-to-do it, there was misinformation, and put downs, pseudo-science in place of the real thing, the promotion of alchemy and bullshit over peer review and experience.

What sealed its fate was the appearance of a cult of personality. That and ego got in the way of useful information. The rot set in and spread fast. I am ashamed that we let it happen, and sad that trusting what one reads in online diving forums isn't as safe as it once was.

Of course, diving a tiny victim. The rot has spread much further. Marianna Spring is the BBC's Disinformation & Social Media Correspondent. Her job is to ferret out what's dodgy and pull it kicking and screaming into daylight in the hope that light will eventually make it shrivel and die. She pokes the trolls, and challenges conspiracy theorists.

For her trouble, she's had her life threatened: often. She's been bullied: repeatedly. She's been defamed: almost daily. One of her anti-fans is Elon Musk.

She's good at her job.

But she works waist-deep in Ben Elton's 'vast sewer of ignorance,' where a TV and radio network feels the need to hire a person whose job is basically to point out to its listeners who the liars are, because it's become close to impossible to tell.

Online life imitates art and we have allowed it to become as indecipherable as the Marvel Multiverse where villains and good guys are one amorphous mass.

So, if you want to find out about diving, the best solution: read books, find a mentor, go diving!

ADMITTING TO MISTAKES AND NEAR MISSES

Kintsugi is a traditional method of repairing a bowl or teacup or any piece of ceramic that's chipped or cracked or broken into pieces and then glued back together again. However, the seams – the joins and any holes left by missing chips – are made purposely very visible.

The fixing process is performed using a paste of Japanese lacquer mixed with gold powder. The effect is truly beautiful, so much so that punters like me, have been known to buy a perfectly good bowl (Japanese or Pueblo in this house), smash it with a hammer (a small toffee hammer works well), and have it repaired to be displayed as a piece of art.'

I don't know the history of *Kintsugi,* but I think I know what it means. Not the word *Kintsugi* (which just means *gold seams*), but the thinking, the philosophy, behind it.

It features in one of many Zen stories about value I was taught as a young man, like this one.

It's said that a powerful magistrate bought a very expensive ceramic vase and displayed in prominently in the hallway of his home. A home filled with expensive treasures. When a visiting Buddhist abbot looked at his new vase and ignored it, saying nothing at all about how beautiful it was, the magistrate was fuming. He was so angry, that as soon as the monk left, he picked up the vase and threw it to the floor smashing it to pieces.

The next day, the vase, now pieced back together with lacquer and gold dust by a servant, was back on its pedestal in the front hall. And, of course, the abbot once again walked into the magistrate's home, but on this visit, he praised the vase telling the magistrate it was one of the most wonderful things in his house.

The story, being Zen, has several lessons to teach. On one level, when something has been broken and fixed, it gains special status. In this case, the servant thought the vase had sufficient worth to warrant the trouble of putting it back together: and putting it back in its place. The servant recognised its 'Buddha nature' and the effort and skill that went into creating it. They celebrated and showed respect for those things by fixing it.

Lesson two. The act of making something whole again —
based on Buddhist values — is an example of applying what it is one
practices while meditating to the small things in everyday life:
mindfulness in action. Anyone who's done a jigsaw puzzle gets a
sense of what that means. One loses self.

And then again, the obvious repairs traced across the body
of the vase, while adding additional visual appeal, are also a
reminder of the correlation between magistrate's pride and the
anger that caused him to smash an expensive object.

One could also argue that the vase in its repaired state
illustrates 'life truths' recognised in Zen: everything in life is
impermanent and changing (nothing lasts); possessing things doesn't
make you happy (it's a zero-sum game), there is no eternal perfect
self (no soul and no ego).

We could possible find more. However, regardless of all that
the vase becomes an object lesson in the relationship between
cause and effect.

And there is something tucked away in there that divers can
learn from.

A friend involved in diver education and the relationship
between undesired outcomes and human nature, says that we (the
diving community) misunderstand an invaluable resource.
Sometimes. we fail to fully understand what we don't do has a
potential effect far greater than what we do, do.

Often, in diving, near misses (seriously bad things that could
have happened but somehow didn't) are often treated as successes.
We celebrate when we should be learning. Imperfections in our

diving, our failure to plan, or our inability to admit we screwed up, are an opportunity for us to reflect and understand limitations. Brushing this opportunity aside, choosing to ignore that 'the vase is broken and needed to be fixed, can lead us to a normalisation of the risks that we face.

Gareth Lock, the founder of *The Human Diver* gives an excellent example of this describing a diving instructor with four students on a basic course. His boss (the dive-store owner) asks him to take care of a certified diver who is getting in an extra dive to complete a different program and familiarise themself with new dive gear. "Not a big deal."

However, the instructor is so task-loaded with his students (who all do very well), that he doesn't notice the extra diver is having issues and when the group surfaces that diver has very little gas in his cylinder. Or that particular diver when realizing his gas is dangerously low doesn't signal anyone because he doesn't want to disrupt the class.

On a superficial level, the dive was fine: even successful. Everyone is out of the water and there's no foul.

But so much was wrong and it's only a wing and a prayer that kept it from going completely pear-shaped. First the store-owner's decision to 'take care of a certified diver,' while the instructor had a class to look after is completely insane. He is condemning that single diver to dive without a buddy and completely alone. The diver had issues that could have cost him his life. The dive store owner needs to rethink what he thinks of as safe practice.

Both the instructor and the diver who was diving alone, should have realised the potential for failure. There is nothing in the instructor manual or diving guidelines that says it's okay to tag along on a class when you're getting used to new gear.

All in all, as far as Lock's example goes, the vase is totally broken and not noticing is a huge, missed opportunity to fix it.

Lock writes: "The research indicates that if we have a 'successful' outcome following a near-miss, then our perception of the risk is lowered, and therefore we are more likely to erode the safety margins that we have developed through training, equipment configurations, standards, and 'rules'. This has been likened to a 'Normalisation of Deviance' – note that a Normalisation of Deviance isn't just about the deviance, but also the social acceptance of the deviance (or reduction in risk margins)."[10]

Perhaps those of us who are blessed with unending good luck can ignore the lessons of surviving a near miss. The rest of us mustn't fall into that trap. Surviving is too good a learning opportunity to let it pass. However, the learning must start with a thorough be-brief and an honest assessment and close inspection of all the dive's cracks and seams.

++

NITROGEN UNDER PRESSURE: SO MANY VARIABLES

If you're a farmer, a gardener, a chemistry major, or a diver, you will be on first-name terms with nitrogen.

It's a gas that, by volume, makes up around 78 percent of the air surrounding us right now. Nitrogen has no smell, taste, or colour.

---

[10] Gareth Lock's excellent blog can be found at *www.thehumandiver.com*

Although it sounds like a total nonentity, without it plants wouldn't thrive, animals simply wouldn't exist, and this planet of ours would be a lifeless lump of rock whizzing around the sun, barefaced and sad.

However, because of nitrogen, we have lots of green plants and algae, fertilizers, food preservatives, refrigerants, an electronics industry, mild anesthetics, annealed steel, and problems for SCUBA divers.

Atmospheric nitrogen, that colourless, odorless gas, is at the heart of several issues for divers when it's breathed under pressure. At blame is the weight of water, which of course increases as a diver goes deeper and deeper in the water column. Actually, the blame is the weight of water plus the atmospheric pressure pushing down on the water's surface.

This requires that any gas a diver breathes to be compressed, therefore that gas is denser, therefore, more of it enters a diver's lungs, and, without going down too deep a rabbit hole and delving into various gas laws, the partial pressures of each component gas filling the lungs increases: so, the dose goes up.

Atmospheric pressure varies a little depending on weather, but 101,325 pa or 1013.25 millibars is pegged as normal. Unless they are driving a boat and being mindful of the surprise arrival of storm fronts, divers ignore swings of a handful of millibars one way or the other. Recreational diving's needs, far from a scientific when it comes time to measure things, are satisfied by calling atmospheric pressure one bar – or one atmosphere in some parts of the world – rather than going to the trouble of tracking millibars or pascals.[11]

Conveniently, water pressure doesn't change since water isn't compressible – not at recreational diving depths at least – so the pressure it exerts is lineal: one bar for every ten metres of seawater; very slightly more for freshwater. Therefore, at 50 metres, the ambient pressure would be roughly six bar (five for water pressure and one for the air pressure at the surface).

And it's the changes in pressure on a diver's body that disrupts body tissues creating issues for the unfortunate, uninformed., and unlucky.

Both barotrauma and arterial gas embolism are due to the expansion, or compression of gas filled spaces within a diver's body. These include lungs, sinuses, gut, teeth in need of dental work, and middle ears. In some cases, these injuries would be life altering, or life ending. But more commonly, they're uncomfortable.

Decompression Sickness, which is the rapid release of dissolved nitrogen (or helium) in supersaturated blood and other body tissues. This is the most interesting effect of the lot. As divers travel deeper and swim around longer at depth, any gas they breathe other than oxygen is dissolved in their blood and body tissues putting them at risk of serious complications during their ascent back to the surface.

---

[11] Perhaps it's worth noting that some compensations are made when diving in mountain lakes since atmospheric pressure lessens at altitude. If you've driven over mountains, you've probably noticed your ears 'popping' because of pressure changes.

If all this sounds like enough to keep anyone but the insane and foolhardy away from SCUBA , workable fixes are basic, simple, and taught in every open water level class worth its price of entry. Plus, the most baffling, most complex – and subject of countless books, and articles – decompression sickness, is managed very cleverly by modern, late-generation personal dive computers.[12]

But the 'nitrogen effect' of increased pressure for divers at depth is nitrogen narcosis. It's interesting, most often misunderstood and misrepresented by divers and non-divers alike. Its symptoms are commonly compared to drinking martinis. One martini for every 10 metres of depth.

And if your taste for booze doesn't sync with James Bond, substitute each martini with drinking shots of tequila with beer chasers. The deeper you go, the more blitzed you become.

I am not a keen supporter of this alcoholic drinks comparison because it trivialises the latent seriousness of narcosis and paints an entirely wrong picture.

For example, many of us enjoy a drink, and for most it's a social norm. For example, at a special dinner, with an uber on call after to get us home, an aperitif, a couple of glasses of wine during the meal wouldn't result in a being blitzed. For most of us, that much booze wouldn't raise many idiomatic eyebrows. But at depth on SCUBA, it doesn't happen like that. It's more like standing at the bar and knocking back three shooters within twenty or thirty seconds. The onset of narcosis is neither enjoyable nor particularly social.

---

12 Time to plug Shearwater Research of Richmond, BC, Canada, who have made an excellent range of products that are a popular choice for many SCUBA , CCR, and freedivers.

Under the influence of narcosis, people show very poor judgment and become disoriented and often euphoric. The Coles Notes version is that a 'narced' diver can become irrational with markedly slower reaction times, which puts themselves and their buddies at risk.

There are no stats that I can find that explain why so many new divers do silly things like running so low on gas that the last few minutes of their dives are frantic and less than relaxing, but I'd put money on narcosis being the issue behind it.

The textbooks suggest for divers breathing air, narcosis becomes noticeable at 30 metres or less. The narcotic hit from breathing compressed air at 90 meters, would be so strong, the majority of us would pass out.

The usual way to manage the effects of narcosis for divers heading to 30 metres or greater is to add helium to their cylinders because helium does not cause narcosis. It brings its own issues during ascent, which broadly speaking has to be slower than when breathing compressed air or nitrox, and when travelling to great depths, well beyond the scope of recreational or even advanced technical diving, it can affect a diver's nervous system.

Two other factors when diving with helium are that in the last decade, the price of helium has increased exponentially, and it simply is not readily available everywhere.

OXYGEN NARCOTIC OR NOT?

One serious misunderstanding is that although nitrogen partial pressure at depth is a major factor in narcotic loading, there are several others that magnify its effects. Top of the list is work of breathing (increased buildup of carbon dioxide). This is simply because the density of gas increases as it's breathed further down the water column, and it takes more effort to move it through the regulator first stage.

Studies suggest a 5.2 g/L is a comfortable maximum density for most divers. This corresponds to breathing air at around 30 metres. Cold water, stress (tiredness, unfamiliar dive site, unfamiliar equipment), working hard at depth, poorly serviced regulators – or a badly designed regulator – poor visibility, and certain drugs (over the counter, prescription, and recreational) are additional factors that can increase the effects of narcosis.

There is anecdotal evidence that a diver's susceptibility to narcosis is not a constant and its effects can swing from minor, through moderate, all the way to major for the same person, with all variables the same, including depth, from one day to another.

A few divers believe that they feel less 'narced' breathing nitrox (a breathing gas with more oxygen and therefore less nitrogen).

Perhaps a good lesson on exactly how much of a moving target narcosis is, and how poorly understood the issue is, there's no consensus on whether the science suggests this is possible or not. The Meyer–Overton hypothesis is the theory of anaesthetic action of a gas relates to its lipid solubility.

Oxygen is more so than nitrogen. Confused? So, are the major training agencies.

CMAS, RAID, GUE, and PADI and include oxygen as equivalent to nitrogen in their equivalent narcotic depth (END) calculations. PSAI considers oxygen narcotic but less so than nitrogen. Others like BSAC, IANTD, NAUI and TDI teach their students that oxygen is not narcotic.

ONE FINAL NOTE

It would be remiss to end an essay on the effects of breathing compressed gas at depth without mentioning another concern about oxygen even though nitrogen is the main player in our little saga.

Oxygen toxicity is function of breathing a gas too rich in oxygen deeper than one should. For pure oxygen, this is around six metres, for air (about 21 percent oxygen) it's around 66 metres. This malady comes in three forms depending on exposure times and oxygen partial pressure (dose), plus individual susceptibility: neurologic, pulmonary, and ocular. Neurologic (AKA central nervous system or CNS) oxygen toxicity is the most common manifesting itself at depth as a tonic-clonic seizure.

Question Nineteen

DO YOU STILL DIVE REBREATHERS? I ONLY SEE MENTION OF OPEN CIRCUIT DIVES IN YOUR BLOG AND SOCIAL MEDIA POSTS RECENTLY?

I started working with rebreathers primarily to dive on historically interesting shipwrecks sitting in four-degree water deep in North America's Great Lakes. When it came time to choose the right tool for that job, rebreathers won the bid. They excel when lots of helium is called for, when the workload is moderate, and warm, moist gas – which is exactly what a rebreather delivers – makes for a comfortable dive. Most of my diving now is in shallow caves, filled with warm water, and the advantages of closed-circuit technology are secondary to the convenience and relative simplicity of aluminum tanks, a pair of high-performance regulators, and a Shearwater computer.

Most of us are familiar with images of Jacques-Yves Cousteau and his *Calypso* crew members, swimming among coral heads, surrounded by fish with clouds of exhaled bubbles tracing their way to the surface. Who could have guessed that his modifications of Emile Gagnan's demand regulator (invented as a work-around for gasoline shortages in Nazi-occupied France, by the way) would trigger *Sea Hunt*, the charmed life of treasure hunter Mel Fisher, Eugenie Clark's ground-breaking research into shark behaviour, and Jacqueline Bisset's unusual choice of thermal protection in the movie *The Deep*.

However, for me, Hans and Lottie Hass delivered the message that diving was sexy and cool. This Austrian couple had a show on BBC TV when I was a nipper. It was such a revelation that I was hooked from episode one.

To film their underwater adventures, Hans and Lottie used a homemade housing for a 16mm Arriflex movie camera and rebreathers – a technology that predated open-circuit, compressed-air devices of Yves Le Prieur and Cousteau.

No bubbles.[13]

THIS IS A CCR

A Closed-Circuit Rebreather (CCR) is a simple system: a bag of gas, a chemistry set to remove carbon-dioxide, a system to squirt a little oxygen into the bag of gas, another system to add a gas to dilute the oxygen and compensate for pressure as the diver goes deeper, and an array of sensors and displays to show the diver what gas they're

---

[13] In fact, Hans and Lottie used what's called an SCR which is a version of rebreather that actually does occasionally release a burp of exhaled gas, so there are bubbles but nothing like as many as on conventional SCUBA .

breathing. No bubbles, far less noise, which allows a much closer approach to marine life if that's your bag, and plenty of other advantages over regular SCUBA .

The most extraordinary is how little gas is needed to keep a diver happy at depth. The deeper one goes, the more remarkably economical a CCR becomes since instead of the exhaled gas leaving the diver's mouthpiece and forming clouds of bubbles streaming to the surface, it's directed into a counterlung (the fancy name for the bag of gas), where it is scrubbed clean of carbon-dioxide. Then a tiny volume of oxygen is added to replace what the diver metabolised, and the result – clean gas – is delivered back to the diver to rebreathe.

On open circuit SCUBA gear, a diver use around 12-14 litres of gas per minute at surface pressure. As they go deeper, they need to breathe more to compensate for the pressure that the surrounding water exerts on their body.

For instance, at 40 metres, that pressure is five times what it is on the surface and so 12-14 litres of gas per minute becomes 60-70 litres per minute.

Oddly, the volume of oxygen that our body needs to stay alive (to metabolise), is more or less constant regardless of depth. It varies a bunch from person to person, but a fair guesstimate is 1.5 litres a minute. All the rest is just needed to overcome the pressure pushing on the person's body.

So, of the 60-70 litres a diver breathes at 40 metres, about two percent is metabolised, the rest is exhaled and launched into the water column to form a pretty reverse cascade of bubbles racing to the surface. On a rebreather, all that gas is collected in the counterlungs and recycled.

The end result is that a rebreather diver uses a fraction of the gas that an open-circuit diver would need to make a comparable dive. When one of the component gases in a breathing mix is helium – used to lessen the effects of narcosis, and the work of breathing at depth – filling a dive cylinder can be astonishingly expensive since helium suitable for diving costs at least two or three Euros per litre!

IT'S ALL DOWN TO THE SCRUBBER

A quick word about the process of removing carbon dioxide from the gas a diver breathes out. It's channeled into a "scrubber" packed with a 'soda lime' compound that contains sodium hydroxide, calcium hydroxide and enough water to facilitate a reaction. As the exhaled gas works its way through the scrubber, a three-part chemical reaction removes the carbon dioxide, creates heat, a bunch more water, and calcium carbonate.

So, the end result is warm, well hydrated gas leaves the scrubber and the rebreather checks the oxygen content matches what the diver set it to, adjusts as necessary, and the diver breathes in.

That's a mite simplified, there are variations, and rebreathers come in all shapes and sizes. Some are totally computerised with oxygen levels monitored and automatically adjusted, other gases checked, and levels displayed (including carbon dioxide), many have various quick shutoffs and manual overrides built in. Others are bog-standard and totally manually operated: no computers in sight. As simple as shooting the north star on a calm, cloudless night.

However, while some have stacks of bells, whistles, and gongs, the basic function is the same regardless.

So, rebreathers are cool, and, if set-up correctly, operated as per the owner's manual, serviced according to schedule, and nothing goes wrong, because no shortcuts or quick assumptions were made, rebreathers are a breeze to dive. If not, they are as user-friendly as a Sainsbury's shopping bag filled with rattlesnakes.

According to stats published at Rebreather Forum 4 (a dive industry event held in Malta in 2023) there are 24 recreational CCR manufacturers. Some with a single model on the market, others with two, three, or more. This makes for a fragmented market for consumers and distorts consumer perception. For example, DAN research director, Dr Frauke Tillmans, estimated at that time there were between 25,000 and 35,000 rebreather units in use today.[14] This is an astonishing finding.

So, does this make them mainstream? Certainly, one sees more and more CCRs at dive sites, but according to data released at RF4, CCR safety remains a serious concern and, according to one source) the estimated risk of dying on a rebreather at 5-10 times higher than that on open-circuit SCUBA .

THE RISKS ARE NOT TRIVAL

Bluntly, until those stats change, CCRs can never be considered mainstream. The average punter is not going to play a zero-sum game weighted that heavily against them. Especially when there is

---

[14] I call bullshit on these numbers. At an average retail cost of $10,000 and taking the middle ground on the number of units in use, the retail value of the CCR market comes out to around $300,000,000. And it simply isn't that high.

also a sticker shock factor at play. On average, a CCR unit in a basic configuration comes with a €7,100 / $10,500 price tag.

However, all this aside, the deciding factor for me to sell my rebreathers (I owned several) and switch to old-school, multi-cylinder sidemount, was something else.

The extra risk, additional cost, and complexity of CCR diving doesn't gel with the type of diving I chose to do right now. That will change at some point. But CCR is not the right tool right now.

There's plenty of scope for something nasty to happen on a rebreather dive. A CCR is an epic tool, but it's not fit for every purpose. For example, one does not need a Vacheron Constantin wristwatch to make sure you roll-up on time for a date for a tax audit. And it's probably not the best choice of personal jewelry for that particular appointment: especially if you intend to plead poverty.

The cave dives I do now, can be managed quite comfortably with a Swatch. Hold on, not a swatch. That wouldn't be kosher. Let's say a TAG.

Additionally, to operate a CCR efficiently and as close to safely as possible, one has to use it frequently: at least twice a month, better yet, twice a week. I no longer have that kind of diving schedule.

So, the answer is simple. CCRs are a great tool for divers whose mission justifies the benefit/risk analysis, and who find themselves called upon to make those specific dives, several times a month.

My current disfavour with diving CCRs may change. If I get invited on an expedition to the Britannic or some other historic, exceedingly deep site that's worth the effort and that triggers the desire to go to the trouble of ramping up for a 'special date,' who knows. Perhaps all current bets will be off.

But for now, I'm just an old grey-haired dude who hangs around in caves looking at jaw-dropping scenery with a regulator instead of a BOV stuck in his mouth.

About The Author

Canadian explorer, Steve Lewis was a respected instructor for cave and other technical programs for many years. He is now instructor emeritus and VP of Marketing for a SCUBA and freediving certification agency based in the UK but with regional offices, and hundreds of dive operations, around the world. A fellow of the Royal Canadian Geographical Society, recipient of a several awards, he remains an avid cave diver with a special interest in Paleoindian and the pre-Columbian culture of the Americas. He lives part-time in Mexico; and the remainder of the year traveling or splitting residency between a restored 19th-century schoolhouse in rural Ontario and a much more regular home in a suburb of Metropolitan Toronto. He and his partner seem to attract regular-sized cats and giant dogs, hence, bedlam rules regardless of where he is. He has published more than one hundred articles and several books on diving including the best-selling *Six Skills and Other Discussions*.

Index

A LINEMARKER PRODUCTION

www.ingramcontent.com/pod-product-compliance
Lightning Source LLC
Chambersburg PA
CBHW051822090426
42736CB00011B/1605